Bhakti
An Religious

by

Anup Singh

Bhakti

An Religious

by Anup Singh

ISBN: 978-93-61420-04-7

Published by

DOUBLE 9 BOOKS

2/13-B, Ansari Road
Daryaganj, New Delhi – 110002
info@double9books.com
www.double9books.com
Tel. 011-40042856

ABOUT THE AUTHOR

The author of this book is Anup Singh and this is going to be his first published book but he has written a lot of books in this few years but not published them. Anup Singh has also a good knowledge of authors and their books. He was also the editor of this book and he has a good knowledge of how to format a book and how to edit them. He was a certified author from Som Bhatla author's Academy and he also crecked the exam of National Author's Academy batch 2021-22, through his talent of writing, Anup Singh is able to be a Published Author from an experienced Author.

CONTENTS

PREFACE

India, a land of diverse cultures and traditions, is celebrated for its vibrant festivals that reflect the rich tapestry of its heritage. The multitude of festivals in India not only adds a kaleidoscope of colors to its cultural landscape but also fosters a sense of unity and togetherness among its people. This book offers a glimpse into the top 12 festivals of India.

-Anup Singh

INTRODUCTION

India, a kaleidoscope of traditions and cultures, is a land where festivities echo the vibrant spirit of its people. The country boasts a tapestry of festivals, each woven with its own unique colors, customs, and significance. From the resplendent lights of Diwali to the jubilant hues of Holi, and the solemnity of Eid al-Fitr, India's festivals embody the essence of unity in diversity. In this exploration, we delve into the heart of India's cultural celebration, shining a spotlight on the top six festivals that encapsulate the nation's rich heritage and diverse religious traditions. These festivals are not merely events on the calendar; they are reflections of India's collective identity, where traditions blend seamlessly with modern celebrations, creating a mosaic of joy and communal harmony. Join us on this journey through the enchanting world of India's top festivals, where each celebration unfolds a unique chapter of cultural magnificence. This book covers top 12 festivals of India. That are-

1. Durga Puja
2. Diwali
3. Holi
4. Ganesh Chaturthi
5. Eid
6. Chhath Puja
7. Vaishaki
8. Makar Sankranti
9. Christmas
10. Raksha Bandhan
11. Jhanmastami
12. Onam

I
DURGA PUJA

May Maa Durga empower you with her 9 blessings of name, fame, health, wealth, happiness, humanity, knowledge, devotion and power.

Kreeti Chinta

Durga Puja: A Grand Celebration of Goddess Durga in India

scriptures. The earliest references to Durga worship can be found in the Puranas, which are ancient Hindu texts. The earliest known Durga Puja in Bengal dates back to the late 16th century, but it was not as grand and elaborate as the modern-day celebrations.

The transformation of Durga Puja into the grand spectacle it is today is attributed to the efforts of the Raja (king) of Krishnanagar, Maharaja Nabakrishna Deb. In the 18th century, he initiated a public celebration of

Durga Puja, also known as Durgotsava, is one of the most significant and grand festivals celebrated in India, primarily in the state of West Bengal. It is dedicated to the worship of Goddess Durga, a powerful and divine embodiment of the feminine force, representing the victory of good over evil. The festival is not only a religious event but also a cultural extravaganza that unites people, transcending boundaries and backgrounds. This celebration spans over several days and involves intricate rituals, elaborate decorations, artistic expressions, and a deep sense of community participation. In this essay, we will explore the various aspects of Durga Puja, its history, significance, customs, and its role in Indian society.

Historical Background

Durga Puja has a long and fascinating history that dates back to ancient times. It is believed that the worship of the goddess Durga can be traced to the earliest Hindu scriptures. The earliest references to Durga worship can be found in the Puranas, which are ancient Hindu texts. The earliest known Durga Puja in Bengal dates back to the late 16th century, but it was not as grand and elaborate as the modern-day celebrations.

The transformation of Durga Puja into the grand spectacle it is today is attributed to the efforts of the Raja (king) of Krishnanagar, Maharaja Nabakrishna Deb. In the 18th century, he initiated a public celebration of Durga Puja to unite the community and promote social harmony. This marked the beginning of the community Durga Puja celebrations that are now the hallmark of the festival.

Significance of Durga Puja

Durga Puja holds immense religious and cultural significance. From a religious perspective, it symbolizes the victory of Goddess Durga over the demon Mahishasura, who threatened to plunge the world into chaos. The goddess is depicted as a fierce warrior riding a lion and wielding various weapons. Her triumph over evil is seen as a representation of the victory of good over evil, and the festival serves as a reminder of the importance of righteousness and justice in life.

Culturally, Durga Puja is a unifying force. It brings people together regardless of their social, economic, or cultural backgrounds. The festival transcends religious boundaries, and people from various communities actively participate in the celebrations. It is a time when the entire community comes together to build and worship the magnificent idols, visit the beautifully decorated pandals (temporary temples), and enjoy cultural performances.

Preparations for Durga Puja

Durga Puja is a festival that demands extensive preparations and planning. It begins months in advance, with committees formed to oversee various aspects of the celebration. The major steps in preparing for Durga Puja include:

1. **Idol Making**: The process of making the idols of Goddess Durga and her children, Saraswati, Lakshmi, Kartikeya, and Ganesha, is a highly specialized and artistic endeavor. Talented artisans and sculptors are entrusted with the task of creating the idols, which are usually made from clay. The idol-making process involves intricate details and craftsmanship.
2. **Pandal Construction**: Elaborate temporary temples or pandals are constructed to house the idols. These pandals are known for their artistic and creative designs. Various themes are chosen each year to decorate the pandals, and committees compete to create the most impressive and innovative designs.
3. **Artistic Decorations**: The entire city is adorned with colorful lights, flowers, and artistic decorations. The streets and buildings are transformed into a magical and festive atmosphere. The decorations play a significant role in creating the ambiance of the festival.
4. **Cultural Programs**: Durga Puja is not just about religious rituals; it is also a platform for cultural expression. Cultural committees organize a variety of programs, including traditional dances, music, drama, and art exhibitions. These events add an element of entertainment and cultural enrichment to the festival.
5. **Food and Feast**: Traditional Bengali cuisine is an integral part of Durga Puja. People indulge in a variety of delectable dishes, including sweets like sandesh and rasgulla. The community organizes feasts, or "bhogs," which are served to the public, emphasizing the spirit of sharing and togetherness.
6. **Community Participation**: Durga Puja is a community-driven festival, and it thrives on the active involvement of

the people. Volunteers from the community come together to manage various aspects of the celebration, from organizing events to ensuring the safety and security of the public.

The Festival Itself

Durga Puja is celebrated over a period of four to five days, with the most important days being Mahalaya, Shashthi, Maha Saptami, Maha Ashtami, Maha Navami, and Dashami. The sequence of events during Durga Puja is as follows:

1. **Mahalaya**: Mahalaya marks the beginning of the festival. It is a time when people pay homage to their ancestors and invite the goddess to descend to Earth. The famous radio program "Mahishasura Mardini," narrated by Birendra Krishna Bhadra, is broadcast on this day, creating a sense of anticipation and excitement.
2. **Shashthi**: On Shashthi, the goddess is welcomed into the pandal, and a symbolic ritual called "Bodhon" is performed. Devotees gather to witness the unveiling of the idol.
3. **Saptami to Navami**: These days are marked by various rituals and cultural performances. The goddess is worshipped with great devotion and fervor. Traditional dances like Dandiya and Dhunuchi Naach are performed during these days.
4. **Maha Ashtami**: Maha Ashtami is one of the most important days of the festival. It involves a series of rituals, including the Kumari Puja, where a young girl is worshipped as the embodiment of the goddess. This day also features the Sandhi Puja, a significant event during which the goddess is believed to have annihilated Mahishasura.
5. **Maha Navami**: On Maha Navami, elaborate rituals continue, and devotees offer their prayers to the goddess. It is also a day for cultural performances and music.
6. **Dashami**: Dashami is the concluding day of Durga Puja. It is a day of farewell to the goddess. Married women offer "Sindoor Khela," where they smear each other with vermillion, and the idols are immersed in water bodies, symbolizing the goddess's return to her divine abode.

Cultural Highlights of Durga Puja

Durga Puja is not just about religious ceremonies but also about cultural celebrations. Some of the cultural highlights of the festival include:

1. **Pandal Hopping**: One of the most popular activities during Durga Puja is "pandal hopping." People visit various pandals to admire the artistic designs and decorations. Each pandal is a unique experience, often built around specific themes that convey social messages or showcase creativity.
2. **Dhunuchi Naach**: This traditional dance form involves dancing with a clay incense burner called a "dhunuchi" while balancing it on one's head. It is performed to the beats of traditional drums and adds a lively and festive atmosphere to the celebrations.
3. **Traditional Music**: Classical and folk music play a vital role in Durga Puja. Traditional instruments like the dhak (a type of drum) are used in various ceremonies. Additionally, artists perform classical music and dance to entertain the crowds.
4. **Art Exhibitions**: Many Durga Puja committees organize art exhibitions to showcase the work of local artists. These exhibitions promote cultural awareness and provide a platform for artists to display their creativity.
5. **Competitions and Awards**: Various awards are presented to the best pandals and idols, encouraging creativity and healthy competition among the organizers. The most prestigious award is the "Sharad Samman," which recognizes excellence in different aspects of Durga Puja.

Social and Economic Impact

Durga Puja has a significant social and economic impact on the communities and regions where it is celebrated. Some of these effects include:

1. **Economic Boost**: Durga Puja leads to a surge in economic activities. Local businesses, artisans, and vendors experience increased sales, and the hospitality industry witnesses a rise in tourism during this time.

2. **Employment Opportunities**: The festival creates employment opportunities for artists, craftsmen, decorators, musicians, and volunteers. It also generates temporary employment in the hospitality and transportation sectors.
3. **Social Bonding**: Durga Puja fosters a sense of community and social bonding. People from diverse backgrounds come together to celebrate the festival. It promotes unity and solidarity among residents.
4. **Cultural Preservation**: Durga Puja plays a pivotal role in preserving and promoting Bengali culture and traditions. It is a platform for artists, musicians, and artisans to showcase their talents and keep the cultural heritage alive.
5. **Promotion of Tourism**: Durga Puja has become a significant draw for tourists, both from within India and internationally. The grandeur of the festival, the artistic displays, and the cultural performances make it a must-visit event for many.

Challenges and Concerns

While Durga Puja is celebrated with great enthusiasm and fervor, it also faces several challenges and concerns:

1. **Environmental Impact**: The immersion of idols made of non-biodegradable materials can lead to pollution in water bodies. In recent years, there has been a shift towards eco-friendly idols made of clay.
2. **Traffic Congestion**: The massive influx of people during the festival can lead to traffic congestion and safety concerns. Adequate measures are taken to manage crowds and ensure safety.
3. **Commercialization**: Some critics argue that the commercialization of Durga Puja has shifted the focus from its spiritual and cultural significance to a more materialistic one.
4. **Financial Burden**: The cost of organizing Durga Puja can be substantial, and some committees face financial challenges. They rely on sponsorships and donations to cover their expenses.

5. **Noise Pollution**: The use of loudspeakers and firecrackers during the festival can contribute to noise pollution, which can be a concern for public health.

CONCLUSION

Durga Puja is a remarkable and multifaceted festival that encapsulates the cultural, social, and religious fabric of India. It is a celebration of the triumph of good over evil, a showcase of artistic creativity, and a platform for cultural expression. Beyond its religious roots, Durga Puja plays a pivotal role in promoting social unity, economic growth, and the preservation of cultural heritage.

In recent years, efforts have been made to address the environmental and logistical challenges associated with the festival, such as the use of eco-friendly idols and crowd management. These changes reflect a growing awareness of the need to balance tradition with sustainability and community welfare.

Durga Puja is a testament to the dynamic nature of Indian festivals, where age-old traditions meet contemporary challenges. It continues to be a source of joy, inspiration, and unity for millions of people, and it remains a shining example of the enduring cultural vibrancy of India.

II
DIWALI

You have to find what sparks a light in you so that you in your own way can illuminate the world.

Parade

Diwali: The Festival of Lights

Diwali, also known as Deepavali, is one of the most celebrated festivals in India and among Indian communities worldwide. It is often referred to as the "Festival of Lights" and holds immense cultural and religious significance. Diwali is a time of joy, merriment, and spirituality, when people come together to celebrate the triumph of light over darkness, good over evil, and knowledge over ignorance. In this essay, we will delve into the history, significance, customs, and the contemporary celebration of Diwali.

Historical and Religious Roots

The origins of Diwali can be traced to various religious and historical contexts, and it is celebrated by multiple faiths, predominantly Hinduism,

Jainism, and Sikhism. While the specific stories and legends may vary, the essence of Diwali remains consistent – it is a celebration of the victory of light and virtue.

One of the most common narratives associated with Diwali is the return of Lord Rama to Ayodhya after defeating the demon king Ravana. According to the epic, Ramayana, Lord Rama, his wife Sita, and his loyal brother Lakshmana returned to Ayodhya after 14 years of exile. The citizens of Ayodhya, overjoyed at their return, illuminated the city with earthen lamps and celebrated the victory of good over evil.

In Jainism, Diwali marks the spiritual awakening of Lord Mahavira, the 24th Tirthankara (spiritual teacher) of Jainism. It is believed that he attained nirvana on the day of Diwali, making it a significant day for the Jain community. Jains engage in prayers, meditation, and worship during this time.

For Sikhs, Diwali, known as Bandi Chhor Divas, commemorates the release of Guru Hargobind Ji from imprisonment in the Gwalior Fort by the Mughal Emperor Jahangir. The Sikhs celebrate this day by lighting lamps and visiting gurdwaras, and it holds both historical and spiritual significance.

Significance of Diwali

Diwali carries multiple layers of significance, and these aspects are deeply ingrained in the cultural and religious fabric of India. Some key elements of its significance include:

1. **Victory of Good over Evil**: The common theme across all Diwali stories is the triumph of good over evil. It serves as a reminder that righteousness and virtue will ultimately prevail, and it inspires individuals to lead a life guided by moral principles.
2. **Symbol of Light and Knowledge**: Diwali is celebrated with the lighting of diyas (oil lamps) and candles. These lights symbolize the removal of darkness and the spread of knowledge. It signifies the dispelling of ignorance and the pursuit of wisdom.
3. **Family and Community Bonding**: Diwali is a time for family and friends to come together. People exchange gifts, visit each other's homes, and share festive meals. The festival strengthens familial and community bonds.

4. **Cleansing and Renewal**: Leading up to Diwali, homes are thoroughly cleaned and adorned with decorations. This practice is not just physical but also spiritual, symbolizing the removal of impurities and the welcoming of positivity and good fortune.
5. **Economic Significance**: Diwali is a major economic event in India. It boosts consumer spending as people purchase new clothes, gifts, and household items. It also marks the beginning of the financial year for businesses and accounts, further emphasizing its economic importance.

Customs and Traditions

Diwali is a multi-day festival that encompasses a variety of customs and traditions. While the specifics may vary by region and community, some common practices associated with Diwali include:

1. **Cleaning and Decorating Homes**: In the days leading up to Diwali, people clean their homes, often referred to as "spring cleaning." Afterward, they decorate their homes with rangoli (colorful designs made with colored powders or rice flour), flower garlands, and decorative lights.
2. **Lighting of Diyas**: The lighting of oil lamps or diyas is one of the most symbolic and visually striking aspects of Diwali. The lamps are placed around homes, temples, and public spaces, illuminating the surroundings and symbolizing the victory of light over darkness.
3. **Prayers and Pujas**: Religious observances are a central part of Diwali. People visit temples and offer prayers to various deities. Special pujas (prayer rituals) are conducted, and offerings are made to seek blessings and guidance.
4. **Exchange of Gifts**: Diwali is a time for giving and receiving gifts. Families and friends exchange presents as a symbol of love and appreciation. It is also customary for employers to give gifts to their employees during this time.
5. **Festive Cuisine**: Special Diwali dishes and sweets are prepared and shared with loved ones. Sweets like ladoos, jalebis, and barfis, along with savory snacks, are a significant part of the festival's culinary delights.

6. **Fireworks and Firecrackers**: Fireworks are a traditional part of Diwali celebrations. The bright bursts of color in the night sky add to the festive atmosphere. However, in recent years, concerns about air pollution and safety have led to calls for more eco-friendly and responsible celebrations.
7. **New Clothes**: Wearing new clothes during Diwali is a custom that signifies renewal and a fresh start. It is believed to bring good luck and happiness.

Contemporary Diwali Celebrations

The way Diwali is celebrated has evolved over time. In contemporary India, the festival has taken on a more modern and global flavor while retaining its traditional essence. Here are some aspects of contemporary Diwali celebrations:

1. **Global Reach**: Diwali is celebrated not only in India but also by Indian communities around the world. It has become a recognized and celebrated festival in countries with a significant Indian diaspora, such as the United States, Canada, the United Kingdom, and Australia.
2. **Eco-Friendly Diwali**: Increasing awareness of environmental issues has led to a shift toward eco- friendly Diwali celebrations. Many people now choose to use eco-friendly and biodegradable diyas and avoid the use of firecrackers to reduce pollution.
3. **Online Shopping and Gifting**: The advent of e- commerce has transformed Diwali shopping. Many people now prefer to shop online, and digital gifting has gained popularity, making it easier for friends and family to exchange gifts.
4. **Diwali Melas and Cultural Events**: Diwali melas (fairs) and cultural events have become a prominent feature of urban celebrations. These events feature live music, dance performances, food stalls, and shopping, providing a festive and community- oriented atmosphere.
5. **Charitable Acts**: Many individuals and organizations use Diwali as an opportunity to engage in charitable acts, such as providing meals to the underprivileged, distributing clothes to the needy, or contributing to social causes.

Challenges and Concerns

While Diwali is a time of great celebration, it is not without its challenges and concerns. Some of the key issues associated with Diwali include:

1. **Air Pollution**: The widespread use of firecrackers during Diwali has been a major contributor to air pollution in India. Concerns over air quality and its impact on public health have led to discussions about limiting firecracker use.
2. **Noise Pollution**: Firecrackers also create high levels of noise pollution, which can disturb people, especially the elderly, children, and pets. Some regions have imposed restrictions on the use of loud fireworks.
3. **Safety Hazards**: Firecrackers can be dangerous if not handled properly. Accidents related to firecrackers are common during Diwali, resulting in injuries and fires. Safety guidelines and regulations have been put in place to mitigate these risks.
4. **Environmental Impact**: The waste generated from the remnants of firecrackers and the pollution caused by their production have adverse environmental consequences. Eco-friendly alternatives are encouraged to reduce this impact.
5. **Commercialization**: The commercialization of Diwali has led to excessive consumerism and materialism. The true spiritual and cultural significance of the festival can be overshadowed by the focus on shopping and consumer spending.

CONCLUSION

Diwali, the Festival of Lights, is a celebration that has transcended time and borders. Its roots in ancient mythology, combined with its modern adaptability, make it a unique and enduring festival. Diwali is not just a religious event; it is a cultural phenomenon that unites people in a spirit of joy, hope, and renewal.

As society grapples with environmental and safety concerns, there is a growing awareness of the need for responsible and eco-friendly Diwali celebrations. The essence of the festival, however, remains unchanged – it is a time to illuminate our lives, dispel darkness, and reaffirm our commitment to good over evil and knowledge over ignorance.

Diwali's universal message of unity, positivity, and enlightenment continues to resonate with people of all backgrounds, making it a festival that not only illuminates homes but also hearts and minds.

III
HOLI

Burn your ego, expectations and ill thoughts in the fire of Holi

Chanting

The Colorful Celebration of Holi: A Festival of Love and Unity

INTRODUCTION

Holi, also known as the Festival of Colors, is one of India's most vibrant and exuberant celebrations. This ancient Hindu festival is celebrated with great enthusiasm and joy throughout the country and has gained popularity in many other parts of the world. Holi signifies the triumph of good over evil, the arrival of spring, and the celebration of love and unity. In this essay, we will explore the rich history, cultural significance, customs, and the spirit of Holi.

Historical Roots of Holi

The origins of Holi can be traced back to ancient India, and its roots are intertwined with various myths and legends. One of the most popular stories associated with Holi is the legend of Prahlad and Holika. Prahlad was a devoted follower of Lord Vishnu, while his aunt Holika, despite being immune to fire, attempted to burn him.

However, due to Prahlad's unwavering faith and Lord Vishnu's protection, Holika was consumed by the flames while Prahlad remained unharmed. This story symbolizes the victory of good over evil and the burning of Holika effigies during Holi celebrations.

Another legend linked to Holi is the story of Radha and Krishna. According to Hindu mythology, Lord Krishna, a mischievous deity, played pranks on the gopis (milkmaids) by drenching them in colored water and smearing them with colored powders. This playful act of Lord Krishna has led to the tradition of throwing vibrant colors on Holi.

Cultural Significance of Holi

Holi has deep cultural and religious significance in India. It marks the arrival of spring, a season associated with rebirth, renewal, and the blossoming of nature. The colorful and joyous celebration of Holi reflects the rejuvenation of life and the welcoming of a new beginning.

Holi is also a time for people to come together, forgive and forget past grievances, and mend broken relationships. It encourages unity and brotherhood, as people from all walks of life celebrate together. The festival transcends social boundaries and brings people of different castes, creeds, and backgrounds under the same colorful umbrella.

Customs and Traditions

Holi is a multi-day festival that involves a series of customs and traditions, each carrying its own unique significance. Let's delve into some of the most prominent customs associated with Holi:

1. Holika Dahan: The night before the main Holi celebration, a bonfire is lit to commemorate the victory of good over evil. People gather around the bonfire, sing songs, and offer prayers. They also throw symbolic items into the fire to represent the destruction of negative forces.
2. Playing with Colors: The most iconic aspect of Holi is the throwing of colored powders and water at each other. Known as "rangwali Holi," this practice symbolizes the

playfulness of Lord Krishna and is a way to express joy, love, and unity. It's a time when social norms and hierarchies are temporarily forgotten.

3. Traditional Sweets: Holi is also a time for culinary delights. Families and communities prepare a variety of traditional sweets, such as gujiya, malpua, and thandai. These delicacies are shared with friends and family, adding to the festive spirit.
4. Music and Dance: Music and dance are integral parts of Holi celebrations. People gather to dance to traditional folk songs and energetic music, often accompanied by drum beats and the melodious tunes of the dholak (a traditional drum).
5. Water Balloons: In some regions, water balloons are a playful addition to the Holi festivities. People fill balloons with colored water and engage in friendly water fights, making the celebration even more enjoyable.

Spirit of Holi

Holi is a festival that exudes happiness, togetherness, and love. It is a time when people let go of their inhibitions and immerse themselves in the joy of colors and camaraderie. The festival promotes unity and a sense of belonging, transcending barriers of age, gender, and social status. Here are some aspects of the spirit of Holi:

1. Expressing Love: Holi is often referred to as the "Festival of Love." It's a day when people express their affection and care for one another by smearing colors, sharing sweets, and embracing in a spirit of love and friendship.
2. Forgiveness and Reconciliation: Holi is an opportunity to bury old grudges and mend broken relationships. It encourages forgiveness and serves as a reminder that love and compassion should prevail over animosity.
3. Breaking Barriers: Holi has the unique ability to bring people from diverse backgrounds together. During the festival, societal hierarchies and norms are temporarily suspended, and everyone becomes equal in the eyes of colors.
4. Joy and Celebration: The sheer exuberance of Holi is infectious. People sing, dance, and play with vibrant colors, letting go of their worries and stress. It's a time for pure, unadulterated joy.

Holi Beyond India

Holi's popularity has transcended borders and cultures, making it a celebrated festival in many parts of the world. In countries like Nepal, Bangladesh, Pakistan, and the Indian diaspora, Holi is embraced with fervor.

Additionally, in recent years, Holi-themed events and festivals have gained popularity in Western countries, allowing people from diverse backgrounds to experience the joy and vibrancy of this Indian festival.

CONCLUSION

Holi, the Festival of Colors, is a testament to the rich cultural heritage and traditions of India. It symbolizes the victory of good over evil, the arrival of spring, and the celebration of love and unity. The customs and traditions associated with Holi are a reflection of the diverse and harmonious nature of Indian society. As the world becomes more interconnected, Holi's appeal is spreading far beyond its traditional borders, carrying its message of love, forgiveness, and unity to people of all backgrounds and cultures. Holi truly encapsulates the essence of celebration, togetherness, and the triumph of joy over negativity.

IV
GANESH CHATURTHI

Ganesha's love is boundless, his blessings infinite.

Anurag Sharma

Ganesh Chaturthi: The Grand Celebration of Lord Ganesha

INTRODUCTION

Ganesh Chaturthi, also known as Vinayaka Chaturthi, is one of the most widely celebrated Hindu festivals in India and around the world. This vibrant and joyous festival is dedicated to Lord Ganesha, the elephant-headed god of wisdom, prosperity, and new beginnings. Ganesh Chaturthi is marked by elaborate preparations, grand processions, and the installation of Ganesha idols in homes and public spaces. In this essay, we will delve into the rich history, cultural significance, customs, and the spirit of Ganesh Chaturthi.

Historical Roots of Ganesh Chaturthi

The origins of Ganesh Chaturthi can be traced back to ancient India. It is believed that this festival was celebrated as early as the 4th and 5th centuries AD. The festival became more prominent and widespread during the Maratha rule in the 17th century, and it gained further recognition during the British colonial period in India.

One of the popular legends associated with the birth of Lord Ganesha and the origin of Ganesh Chaturthi is the story of Parvati, the goddess of power, and Lord Shiva, the god of destruction. According to Hindu mythology, Parvati created Ganesha out of sandalwood paste to guard her while she bathed. When Shiva returned, he was denied entry to his own home by Ganesha, leading to a battle in which Shiva beheaded Ganesha. This act of beheading was a grave mistake, and to console Parvati, Shiva promised to bring Ganesha back to life. He replaced Ganesha's head with that of an elephant, and thus, Lord Ganesha was born.

Cultural Significance of Ganesh Chaturthi

Ganesh Chaturthi holds immense cultural significance in India. It represents the celebration of new beginnings, wisdom, and the removal of obstacles. Lord Ganesha is revered as the remover of hurdles and the deity who blesses his devotees with success and prosperity. People invoke his presence to seek blessings before starting new ventures, educational pursuits, and important life events.

The festival also serves as a symbol of unity and inclusivity, bringing people of all backgrounds and social strata together. It transcends the boundaries of caste, creed, and ethnicity, fostering a sense of community and togetherness.

Customs and Traditions

Ganesh Chaturthi is a multi-day festival with a series of customs and traditions, each holding its own unique importance. Let's explore some of the key customs associated with this grand celebration:

1. Installation of Ganesha Idols: The heart of Ganesh Chaturthi lies in the installation of Ganesha idols. These idols can range from small, household-sized figures to gigantic, community statues. The idols are often made of clay and are meticulously handcrafted by skilled artisans. Once installed, the idols are adorned with vibrant decorations, jewelry, and silk clothing.

2. Prana Pratishtha: Before the idol is installed, a ritual called "Prana Pratishtha" is performed, during which the idol is consecrated with mantras and prayers, infusing it with the divine presence of Lord Ganesha.
3. Daily Pujas and Offerings: Devotees offer daily pujas (ritual worship) to the Ganesha idol during the festival. These pujas include the lighting of oil lamps, the burning of incense, and the offering of sweets, flowers, and coconut. The faithful seek the deity's blessings and guidance in their endeavors.
4. Aarti: Aarti is a traditional ritual of waving a lit lamp in front of the idol, accompanied by devotional songs and chants. It is performed to show reverence and to create a sense of divine connection.
5. Visarjan (Immersion): The culmination of Ganesh Chaturthi involves the immersion of Ganesha idols in water bodies, such as rivers, lakes, or the sea. The immersion signifies the departure of Lord Ganesha and his return to his heavenly abode. This process is accompanied by vibrant processions, music, and dancing.

Spirit of Ganesh Chaturthi

The spirit of Ganesh Chaturthi is a reflection of the essence of Lord Ganesha himself. It embodies wisdom, prosperity, and inclusivity. Here are some aspects of the spirit of Ganesh Chaturthi:

1. Removal of Obstacles: Lord Ganesha is revered as the obstacle remover, and the festival carries the message of seeking his divine intervention to overcome life's challenges. It encourages people to confront hurdles with positivity and determination.
2. New Beginnings: Ganesh Chaturthi is a time for new beginnings, whether it's starting a new business, embarking on an educational journey, or making personal life changes. It symbolizes the clean slate of a fresh start.
3. Community Bonding: The festival fosters a sense of community, as people come together to celebrate, share joy, and seek blessings. It transcends social and economic barriers, uniting people in a common purpose.
4. Art and Culture: The intricate craftsmanship of Ganesha idols, the colorful decorations, and the cultural performances

during the festival showcase India's rich artistic and cultural heritage.

5. Environmental Awareness: In recent years, there has been a growing awareness of the environmental impact of immersing idols made of non- biodegradable materials into water bodies. As a result, eco-friendly Ganesha idols made of clay and natural colors have gained popularity.

Ganesh Chaturthi Beyond India

While Ganesh Chaturthi has its roots in India, its celebration has expanded beyond the country's borders. The festival is now celebrated with enthusiasm by the Indian diaspora in various parts of the world, including the United States, the United Kingdom, Canada, Australia, and many other countries. Indian communities abroad have taken the spirit of Ganesh Chaturthi with them, ensuring that the festival continues to thrive and resonate with generations far from their homeland.

CONCLUSION

Ganesh Chaturthi is a grand celebration that not only honors the elephant-headed god of wisdom and prosperity but also serves as a symbol of new beginnings, unity, and inclusivity. The festival's rich history, customs, and cultural significance make it a deeply cherished and widely celebrated event in India and among the Indian diaspora. As the world becomes

more interconnected, Ganesh Chaturthi's appeal continues to transcend borders, carrying with it the message of wisdom, prosperity, and the power to overcome obstacles and start anew. Ganesh Chaturthi truly encapsulates the essence of devotion, community, and the pursuit of a brighter future.

V
EID

May Allah shower Rahmah upon us and accept our prayers.

Mohamud Rahman

Eid al-Fitr and Eid al-Adha: Celebrating Islamic Festivals

Eid, also spelled as "Eid," is a significant religious festival celebrated by Muslims worldwide. There are two primary Eid festivals in Islam: Eid al-Fitr and Eid al-Adha. These festivals hold immense cultural and religious significance, marking the end of Ramadan, the holy month of fasting, and commemorating the willingness of Prophet Ibrahim (Abraham) to sacrifice his son Isma'il (Ishmael) in obedience to God's command. In this essay, we will explore the history, customs, and the significance of both Eid al-Fitr and Eid al-Adha.

Eid al-Fitr: The Festival of Breaking the Fast

Eid al-Fitr, also known as "Festival of Breaking the Fast," is one of the most important Islamic festivals. It is celebrated at the CONCLUSION of Ramadan, the ninth month of the Islamic lunar calendar, during which Muslims fast from dawn until sunset. This month of fasting is a time of spiritual reflection, prayer, and self- discipline. Eid al-Fitr is a joyous and festive occasion that serves as a reward for the devotion and self-control exhibited during Ramadan.

Historical and Religious Significance

Eid al-Fitr has a deep religious significance in Islam, as it marks the completion of the month-long fasting period. The festival holds spiritual importance, as it is a time of gratitude to Allah (God) for providing the strength and self-control to observe the fast. The history of Eid al-Fitr can be traced back to the time of the Prophet Muhammad, who is reported to have initiated the celebration in Medina after his migration from Mecca.

The term "Eid" means "festival" or "holiday," while "Fitr" means "breaking the fast." Hence, the name signifies the celebration that marks the end of fasting and abstinence. On this day, Muslims come together to offer special prayers and express their gratitude to Allah for the strength and guidance they received during Ramadan.

Customs and Traditions

Eid al-Fitr is celebrated with a series of customs and traditions that vary from region to region, but the following are some common practices associated with the festival:

1. **Sadaqah al-Fitr**: Prior to the Eid prayer, Muslims are encouraged to give to the less fortunate by providing a form of charity known as "Sadaqah al- Fitr." This act of charity is meant to ensure that all Muslims can join in the festivities and experience the joy of Eid.
2. **Eid Prayer**: On the morning of Eid, Muslims gather at mosques or open prayer grounds to offer a special prayer known as "Salat al-Eid." This prayer consists of a sermon and supplication, followed by a short prayer. It is typically performed in congregation, with Muslims dressed in their finest clothes.

3. **Eid Greetings**: People greet each other with the phrases "Eid Mubarak" or "Eid Sa'id," which mean "Blessed Eid" or "Happy Eid." These greetings are exchanged throughout the day, along with warm wishes and hugs.
4. **Eid Feast**: Special meals are prepared and shared with family and friends during Eid. Traditional dishes vary by region but often include a variety of sweet and savory foods. Sweets like baklava, maamoul, and sheer khurma are popular during the celebration.
5. **New Clothes**: It is a tradition to wear new clothes on Eid, signifying the renewal of one's faith and the joy of the occasion. These clothes are often purchased or prepared in advance, and the choice of attire is an important aspect of the festival.
6. **Visiting Relatives and Neighbors**: During Eid, it is customary to visit the homes of relatives, friends, and neighbors to exchange greetings, share meals, and strengthen bonds. This practice promotes a sense of community and unity.
7. **Gift Giving**: Exchanging gifts is a common practice during Eid, especially among family members. Gifts can range from toys for children to clothing, jewelry, or other thoughtful presents for adults.

Eid al-Adha: The Festival of Sacrifice

Eid al-Adha, also known as the "Festival of Sacrifice," is the second major Islamic holiday. It falls on the 10th day of Dhu al-Hijjah, the twelfth month of the Islamic lunar calendar, and it commemorates the willingness of Prophet Ibrahim to sacrifice his son Isma'il in obedience to God's command. Eid al-Adha also coincides with the annual Hajj pilgrimage to Mecca, where millions of Muslims from around the world gather to fulfill one of the Five Pillars of Islam.

Historical and Religious Significance

Eid al-Adha's history is deeply rooted in the story of the Prophet Ibrahim. According to Islamic tradition, Ibrahim had a recurring dream in which he was instructed by Allah to sacrifice his beloved son, Isma'il, as an act of obedience and devotion. The story goes that both father and son willingly submitted to Allah's command, but before the sacrifice could take place, Allah provided a ram to be sacrificed in Isma'il's place. Eid al-Adha commemorates this event as a testament to faith, obedience, and God's mercy.

Customs and Traditions

Eid al-Adha is marked by several customs and rituals that hold significant meaning within Islam:

1. **Sacrifice of Animals**: One of the central customs of Eid al-Adha is the Qurbani, the ritual sacrifice of an animal, usually a sheep, goat, cow, or camel. The act symbolizes the willingness to sacrifice one's possessions and life for Allah. The meat is distributed among family, friends, and the less fortunate.
2. **Eid Prayer**: As with Eid al-Fitr, Muslims gather in mosques or prayer grounds to offer a special prayer, known as "Salat al-Eid." This prayer consists of a sermon and supplication, followed by a short prayer.
3. **Charitable Giving**: In addition to the Qurbani, Muslims are encouraged to perform acts of charity during Eid al-Adha, which may include giving food, clothing, or financial support to those in need.
4. **Eid Greetings**: Similar to Eid al-Fitr, Muslims exchange greetings of "Eid Mubarak" or "Eid Sa'id" to convey well wishes and blessings.
5. **Feasting and Sharing**: As with Eid al-Fitr, a grand feast is an essential part of Eid al-Adha celebrations. The meat from the sacrificed animal is used to prepare delicious dishes and shared with family, friends, and the community.
6. **New Clothes**: As a symbol of renewal and devotion, many Muslims wear new clothes on Eid al-Adha, making a special effort to look their best.
7. **Visiting Relatives**: Just like Eid al-Fitr, Eid al-Adha is an occasion to visit the homes of relatives, friends, and neighbors, promoting community bonding and unity.
8. **Hajj Pilgrimage**: For those fortunate enough to undertake the Hajj pilgrimage, Eid al-Adha has added significance.

It marks the completion of the Hajj and is celebrated by pilgrims in the holy city of Mecca.

Significance of Eid Festivals

Both Eid al-Fitr and Eid al-Adha hold profound religious and cultural significance for Muslims. These festivals represent the following important aspects of the Islamic faith:

1. **Gratitude**: Eid al-Fitr is a time for Muslims to express their gratitude to Allah for the strength and self-control they exhibited during the month of Ramadan. Eid al-Adha serves as a reminder of the importance of submitting to Allah's will, as exemplified by Prophet Ibrahim.
2. **Unity and Brotherhood**: Eid festivals bring the Muslim community together. People from diverse backgrounds gather to pray, exchange greetings, and share meals. These occasions foster a sense of unity, love, and brotherhood among Muslims.
3. **Charity and Generosity**: Both Eid festivals emphasize the importance of charity and generosity. Muslims are encouraged to give to the less fortunate, ensuring that everyone can partake in the festivities and enjoy a special meal.
4. **Spiritual Reflection**: Eid festivals are a time for Muslims to reflect on their faith and their relationship with Allah. It is a time for self- improvement, self-discipline, and renewed spiritual commitment.
5. **Cultural Heritage**: Eid festivals are a celebration of cultural traditions and heritage. The clothing, cuisine, and customs associated with these festivals are unique to each region and contribute to the rich tapestry of Islamic culture.

Challenges and Concerns

While Eid is a time of joy and celebration, it is not without its challenges and concerns:

1. **Animal Welfare**: The sacrifice of animals during Eid al-Adha has raised concerns about animal welfare. Efforts are being made to ensure that the process is humane and adheres to ethical standards.
2. **Environmental Impact**: The practice of animal sacrifice, combined with other festive activities, can have an environmental impact. Managing waste and promoting eco-friendly practices are important considerations.
3. **Commercialization**: In some regions, the commercialization of Eid festivals has led to excessive consumerism and materialism. This can overshadow the religious and cultural significance of the festivals.
4. **Cultural Adaptation**: Muslims living in non-Muslim majority countries may face challenges in celebrating Eid. Efforts are being made to adapt to local customs while preserving the core traditions of the festival.

CONCLUSION

Eid al-Fitr and Eid al-Adha are not only significant religious events but also cultural celebrations that unite Muslim communities across the globe. They encapsulate the essence of Islam, emphasizing faith, unity, gratitude, and charity. These festivals serve as a reminder of the core values of Islam and the importance of family, community, and spirituality.

In a world that often faces division and conflict, Eid festivals offer a message of peace, unity, and the willingness to submit to a higher power. They celebrate the human capacity for faith, compassion, and the pursuit of a better self. As Muslims come together to celebrate Eid, they not only reaffirm their devotion to Allah but also their commitment to the shared values that bind them as a global community.

VI
CHHATH PUJA

May the occasion of Chhath Puja light up new hopes and opportunities in your life and fulfil all your dreams and leave you with a smile.

Shubham Kumar

Chhath Puja: The Ancient Sun Worship Festival of India

Chhath Puja is a significant Hindu festival dedicated to the worship of the sun god, Surya, and Chhathi Maiya, the goddess of energy and consort of Surya. This ancient festival, observed primarily in the Indian states of Bihar, Jharkhand, Eastern Uttar Pradesh, and Nepal, has a deep spiritual and cultural significance. Chhath Puja spans four days and is celebrated with devotion, rigorous rituals, and deep reverence for the sun, which is considered the source of life on Earth. In this comprehensive exploration, we will delve into the history, rituals, significance, and cultural aspects of Chhath Puja.

Historical Roots of Chhath Puja

The history of Chhath Puja dates back thousands of years and is closely associated with the Vedic period. The festival finds mention in the ancient Vedic texts, particularly the Rigveda, where the Sun god, Surya, is extolled for its life-giving properties. The rituals of Chhath Puja are believed to have been initiated by the ancient Dravidians of India. The word "Chhath" originates from the Sanskrit word "Shashthi," which means the number six, as the festival is celebrated on the sixth day of the lunar month after Diwali.

Chhath Puja is a celebration of nature and the sun, recognizing the vital role of the sun in sustaining life on Earth. It is also believed to have mythological roots connected to the epic of Mahabharata, where Draupadi is said to have observed Chhath Puja.

Significance of Chhath Puja

Chhath Puja holds multiple layers of significance, including:

1. **Sun Worship**: At its core, Chhath Puja is a celebration of the sun god, Surya. The sun is revered as the ultimate source of energy, and devotees express their gratitude for the life-sustaining power of the sun.
2. **Harvest Festival**: Chhath Puja coincides with the harvest season, and it is an occasion for farmers to thank the sun god for a bountiful crop. The festival marks the end of the monsoon and the beginning of the harvest season.
3. **Cultural Expression**: Chhath Puja is an integral part of the cultural identity of the people of Bihar and neighboring regions. It fosters a sense of community, cultural bonding, and pride in their traditional customs and rituals.
4. **Austerity and Devotion**: Devotees of Chhath Puja observe strict austerities, including fasting, abstaining from drinking water, and standing in waist-deep water. This showcases their dedication and unwavering faith in the divine.

Rituals of Chhath Puja

Chhath Puja spans four days of rigorous rituals and devotion:

1. **Nahay Khay (Day 1)**: The first day is dedicated to cleaning and purifying the body. Devotees take a dip in a sacred river

or water body before preparing and consuming a simple meal. This meal is known as "kaddu-bhat" and is often made with gourd and rice.

2. **Kharna (Day 2)**: On the second day, devotees observe a day-long fast, abstaining from food and water. In the evening, they prepare thekua, a traditional sweet made from wheat flour, jaggery, and ghee. This is offered to the setting sun, and the fast is broken after the ritual.
3. **Sandhya Arghya (Day 3)**: The third day is the most important of the festival. Devotees gather at the riverbank at dawn and offer prayers to the rising sun. The offering, known as arghya, consists of fruits, sweets, and special offerings like sugarcane, coconuts, and wheat sprouts. The evening ritual, called "Usha Arghya," is dedicated to the setting sun.
4. **Usha Arghya (Day 4)**: On the final day, devotees return to the riverbank before sunrise to offer arghya to the rising sun. This marks the culmination of the Chhath Puja rituals. After the ritual, devotees break their fast with the prasad offered to the sun god.

Cultural Aspects and Celebrations

Chhath Puja is not only a religious festival but also a celebration of culture and community. It brings people together, irrespective of caste, creed, or social status, in a collective display of devotion and reverence for the sun. Some cultural aspects and celebrations associated with Chhath Puja include:

1. **Chhath Ghats**: The riverbanks and water bodies, especially in Bihar and other Chhath-dominant regions, come alive with colorful decorations and temporary pavilions or tents, known as "ghats." These ghats are where the rituals are performed and where devotees congregate.
2. **Chhath Geet**: Chhath Puja is accompanied by traditional folk songs and chants dedicated to the sun god. These songs, known as "Chhath Geet," are an integral part of the celebrations and create a joyous and spiritual atmosphere.
3. **Community Participation**: Chhath Puja is a community affair, and it involves the participation of family members, neighbors, and volunteers who assist in the preparations and rituals. The collective effort reflects the communal spirit of the festival.

4. **Decorations and Offerings**: Chhath Puja involves the use of traditional earthen lamps (diyas), colorful rangoli designs, and decorative items made from bamboo and sugar cane. These decorations, along with the offerings to the sun, create a festive ambiance.
5. **Chhath Processions**: In some regions, grand processions are organized as part of the Chhath Puja celebrations. Devotees, often adorned in traditional attire, carry offerings to the riverbanks accompanied by music and dance.

Chhath Puja Beyond India

Chhath Puja is not limited to India alone. It has transcended geographical boundaries and is observed by the Indian diaspora in various parts of the world, including the United States, the United Kingdom, Canada, Australia, and the Middle East. The festival has gained recognition and respect as a significant cultural and religious celebration.

In Nepal, Chhath Puja is a major festival and holds special importance among the Madhesi and Tharu communities. It is celebrated with fervor and devotion, with rituals similar to those observed in India.

Challenges and Concerns

While Chhath Puja is a deeply cherished festival, it is not without its challenges and concerns:

1. **Environmental Impact**: Chhath Puja rituals often involve immersing items such as sugarcane, coconuts, and earthen lamps in water bodies. This can lead to environmental pollution and degradation, particularly in rivers and lakes.
2. **Safety and Crowd Management**: The large gatherings at riverbanks and ghats during Chhath Puja can present safety challenges. Adequate crowd management and security measures are essential to ensure the well-being of devotees.
3. **Water Pollution**: The practice of taking a dip in rivers can lead to water pollution, especially if water bodies are not adequately protected. Measures to safeguard the water quality and promote cleanliness are necessary.
4. **Public Health Concerns**: The rigorous fasting, standing in water, and exposure to the elements can pose health risks, particularly for the elderly and the young. It is crucial to prioritize public health and safety during the festival.

Conclusion: The Radiant Devotion of Chhath Puja

Chhath Puja is a remarkable celebration that pays homage to the sun, the source of life and energy. It reflects the deep-rooted cultural and spiritual values of the people of Bihar, Jharkhand, Eastern Uttar Pradesh, and Nepal, as well as the Indian diaspora around the world. The festival's significance is not confined to its religious and cultural aspects; it is a powerful symbol of unity, devotion, and reverence for nature.

Chhath Puja embodies the idea of austerity and faith, with devotees undergoing strict rituals and fasts as a testament to their unwavering devotion. The festival's customs and traditions highlight the cultural heritage and shared identity of the communities that observe it.

As with many traditions and celebrations, Chhath Puja faces challenges related to the environment, safety, and public health. In an increasingly interconnected world, there is a growing awareness of the need to adapt and address these concerns while preserving the essence and spirit of the festival.

Chhath Puja is more than a festival; it is a testament to the human capacity for faith, devotion, and the celebration of the life-giving sun. It is a radiant expression of unity, culture, and spirituality that continues to shine brightly in the hearts and minds of those who observe it, and it serves as a source of inspiration and reverence for the power of the sun.

VII
VAISHAKI

May the cheerful spirit of Baisakhi fill your heart with happiness and joy.

-Gobind Singh

Vaisakhi: A Tapestry of Tradition, Celebration, and Unity

INTRODUCTION

Vaisakhi, also known as Baisakhi, holds a special place in the hearts of millions of people around the world. It is a vibrant and joyous festival celebrated by various communities, with its roots deeply embedded in cultural, religious, and historical significance. This comprehensive exploration delves into the origins, religious importance, cultural manifestations, and contemporary celebrations of Vaisakhi, tracing its evolution over centuries and highlighting its enduring relevance.

Historical Roots

Vaisakhi's historical roots can be traced back to the year 1699 when Guru Gobind Singh, the tenth Sikh Guru, founded the Khalsa Panth, a community of initiated Sikhs. This significant event took place on the day of Vaisakhi, marking a turning point in Sikh history. Guru Gobind Singh baptized five volunteers, known as the Panj Pyare, who pledged allegiance to the Sikh principles of equality, justice, and devotion to God. The creation of the Khalsa was a transformative moment that solidified Sikh identity and reinforced the commitment to righteousness and bravery.

Religious Significance

For Sikhs, Vaisakhi is not merely a historical event but a sacred occasion that commemorates the birth of the Khalsa and the unity of the Sikh community. The day holds religious ceremonies, including processions, kirtan (devotional singing), and readings from the Guru Granth Sahib, the holy scripture of Sikhism. Temples, or Gurdwaras, witness a surge in devotees, reflecting the deep spiritual connection that Sikhs feel with Vaisakhi.

Cultural Manifestations

Vaisakhi is not limited to Sikhism; it resonates with various cultural and religious communities. In Punjab, the festival marks the harvest season, symbolizing prosperity and abundance. Farmers express gratitude for the bountiful yield by participating in traditional dances, such as the energetic Bhangra and graceful Gidda. The vibrant colors, lively music, and exuberant dance create an atmosphere of festivity and joy that transcends religious boundaries.

In the broader Indian context, Vaisakhi is celebrated as the New Year in the Hindu solar calendar. It is a time when people clean and decorate their homes, participate in religious rituals, and exchange greetings. The festival encapsulates the spirit of new beginnings, symbolizing hope, renewal, and the cyclical nature of life.

Diversity of Celebrations

Beyond India, Vaisakhi is celebrated by various communities across the globe. Sikh diaspora communities, particularly in countries like Canada, the United Kingdom, and the United States, organize grand processions, Nagar Kirtans, to showcase their cultural heritage and religious devotion. These events bring together people from diverse backgrounds, fostering a sense of unity and understanding.

In Canada, especially in Surrey, British Columbia, the Vaisakhi parade is one of the largest in the world outside of India. The streets come alive with vibrant colors, traditional music, and the aroma of Indian cuisine as thousands gather to celebrate this multicultural spectacle. Politicians, community leaders, and people from all walks of life participate, reflecting the inclusive and diverse nature of Canadian society.

Socioeconomic Impact

Vaisakhi's impact extends beyond its cultural and religious dimensions, significantly influencing the socioeconomic landscape. In agricultural regions like Punjab, the festival is intrinsically linked to the harvest season. Farmers celebrate the abundance of crops and express gratitude for a successful yield. The economic aspect of Vaisakhi is reflected in the purchase of new clothes, jewelry, and gifts during the festivities, contributing to local businesses and markets.

Culinary Delights

No celebration is complete without a culinary extravaganza, and Vaisakhi is no exception. Traditional Punjabi cuisine takes center stage during the festivities, with a plethora of mouthwatering dishes. From the iconic Sarson da Saag and Makki di Roti to the delectable Paneer Tikka and Samosas, the culinary delights of Vaisakhi reflect the richness and diversity of Punjabi culture. Festive meals bring families and communities together, creating a sense of warmth and camaraderie.

Contemporary Relevance

In the contemporary context, Vaisakhi continues to evolve while retaining its core values. The festival has become a platform for social and political discourse, addressing issues such as human rights, equality, and justice. Sikhs worldwide use the occasion to raise awareness about their community's contributions to society and to foster a better understanding of their faith and culture.

The Role of Technology

Technology has played a significant role in shaping the way Vaisakhi is celebrated and experienced. In an era of globalization, live streaming of religious ceremonies allows Sikhs around the world to participate virtually in the festivities. Social media platforms become a powerful tool for sharing cultural insights, connecting with the diaspora, and fostering a sense of community across geographical boundaries.

Challenges and Opportunities

As with any cultural or religious celebration, Vaisakhi faces challenges in the modern world. The commercialization of festivals, cultural appropriation, and the dilution of traditional practices are some concerns that communities grapple with. However, these challenges also present opportunities for communities to reaffirm their cultural identity, educate others about their traditions, and adapt celebrations to resonate with contemporary values.

CONCLUSION

Vaisakhi is a multifaceted tapestry woven with threads of history, spirituality, culture, and community. Its roots may lie in a specific historical event, but its branches have spread far and wide, embracing diversity and fostering unity. As the world continues to change, Vaisakhi stands as a beacon of tradition, celebration, and resilience, reminding us of the enduring power of culture to connect and inspire. In the mosaic of global festivals, Vaisakhi's colors shine bright, inviting people from all walks of life to join in the celebration of life, abundance, and shared humanity.

VIII
MAKAR SANKRANTI

Just as the sun begins its journey towards the north, may your life also take a positive turn towards success and happiness.

-Ayushman Reddy

Makar Sankranti: A Harvest Festival Celebrating Transition and Abundance

INTRODUCTION

Makar Sankranti, a festival celebrated in various parts of India, holds immense cultural, religious, and agricultural significance. Observed on the 14th or 15th of January each year, it marks the transition of the sun into the zodiac sign of Capricorn (Makara). The festival is not only a celestial event but also a time for communities to come together, express gratitude for the harvest, and engage in cultural festivities. This comprehensive exploration delves into the multifaceted aspects of Makar Sankranti, exploring its historical roots, religious connections, cultural expressions, regional variations, agricultural dimensions, and contemporary celebrations.

Historical Roots

Makar Sankranti has ancient roots, dating back to the Vedic period. The festival finds mention in various Sanskrit texts, where the movement of the sun is observed and revered. The shift of the sun into the northern hemisphere, marking longer days and the onset of warmer weather, is celebrated as a time of new beginnings. In Hindu tradition, the Uttarayana, or the northward journey of the sun, begins on Makar Sankranti. This period is considered auspicious, symbolizing the gradual increase of positive energy and divine blessings.

Religious Significance

While Makar Sankranti is primarily a harvest festival, it also holds religious importance in Hinduism. Many devotees take a holy dip in sacred rivers, especially the Ganges, Yamuna, Godavari, and Krishna, to cleanse themselves of sins and seek blessings for the year ahead. The belief is that the sun deity Surya is especially potent during this time, and paying homage to the sun is seen as a form of purification.

In some regions, Makar Sankranti is associated with specific deities. In Maharashtra, it is celebrated as Sankranti and marks the arrival of the sun god Surya in the northern hemisphere. The day is also linked to the legendary figure Bhishma Pitamah from the Mahabharata, who is said to have waited on his deathbed until the auspicious day of Uttarayana to leave his mortal coil.

Cultural Expressions

Makar Sankranti is celebrated with various cultural expressions, each region adding its unique flavor to the festivities. The festival is known by different names in different parts of the country – Pongal in Tamil Nadu, Uttarayan in Gujarat, Lohri in Punjab, Bhogali Bihu in Assam, and Magh Bihu in parts of North India. Each region has its traditional customs, rituals, and culinary delights associated with the celebration.

1. **Makar Sankranti in Gujarat (Uttarayan):**

- Gujarat is renowned for its grand celebrations of Uttarayan. The skies come alive with vibrant kites of all shapes and sizes. The International Kite Festival, held in cities like Ahmedabad and Vadodara, attracts kite enthusiasts from around the world. The entire state engages in friendly kite-flying competitions, making the skies a colorful spectacle.

2. **Pongal in Tamil Nadu:**

- Pongal is a four-day harvest festival in Tamil Nadu, with the main day dedicated to thanking the sun god for a bountiful harvest. The highlight is the preparation of Pongal, a special dish made with freshly harvested rice, milk, jaggery, and other ingredients. Homes are adorned with kolams (decorative patterns made with rice flour) to welcome prosperity.

3. **Lohri in Punjab:**

- Lohri, celebrated a day before Makar Sankranti, is a winter harvest festival in Punjab. Bonfires are lit, and people gather around to offer prayers and perform traditional folk dances like Bhangra and Gidda. The festival is also associated with the tradition of singing Lohri songs and offering sesame seeds and jaggery to the fire.

4. **Bhogali Bihu/Magh Bihu in Assam:**

- Bhogali Bihu, also known as Magh Bihu, is celebrated in Assam to mark the end of the harvesting season. Bonfires, feasts, and traditional Assamese dance forms like Bihu dance are integral to the celebrations. People exchange traditional sweets called pithas and participate in various community activities.

Regional Variations

Makar Sankranti is celebrated with diverse regional variations, each adding its unique charm to the festival. The southern states of India, including Karnataka and Andhra Pradesh, celebrate the day with colorful rangoli, special prayers, and feasts. In Maharashtra, kite-flying competitions and the preparation of special dishes like tilgul (sesame and jaggery sweets) are common traditions.

In West Bengal, Makar Sankranti is known as Poush Sankranti, and people take holy dips in the Ganges. The festival is associated with the deity Goddess Saraswati, and devotees perform puja and cultural programs. In Odisha, the day is celebrated as Makar Mela, and people take part in fairs, cultural events, and kite-flying.

Agricultural Dimensions

Makar Sankranti has deep agricultural roots, signifying the end of the winter harvest and the beginning of longer days with more sunlight. In many parts of the country, farmers express gratitude for the abundance of crops and pray for a prosperous year ahead. The festival is a moment of respite for farmers who have toiled in their fields, and it symbolizes the cyclical nature of agriculture.

The association of Makar Sankranti with the harvest is reflected in the rituals performed during the festival. In some regions, the first harvested grain is offered to the deities, symbolizing thanksgiving and seeking blessings for future crops. The use of sesame seeds, jaggery, and other harvested produce in traditional sweets and dishes adds to the agricultural significance of the festival.

Contemporary Celebrations

In the contemporary context, Makar Sankranti continues to be celebrated with zeal and enthusiasm. While traditional customs and rituals are maintained, new elements are introduced to make the festival more inclusive and appealing to younger generations.

1. **Kite Festivals:**

- Kite festivals have gained immense popularity during Makar Sankranti, especially in states like Gujarat and Rajasthan. These festivals attract participants and spectators from across the country and the world. The artistry and skill involved in kite-flying competitions have turned these events into major tourist attractions.

2. **Social Media and Makar Sankranti:**

- Social media platforms play a significant role in connecting people during Makar Sankranti. The sharing of festive moments, traditional recipes, and artistic kite designs on platforms like Instagram and Facebook allows people to participate virtually and learn about different regional celebrations.

3. **Eco-Friendly Celebrations:**

- There is a growing awareness of the environmental impact of festivals, including the use of plastic in kite strings. Many communities are now promoting eco-friendly celebrations, encouraging the use of biodegradable materials for kites and minimizing waste during the festivities.

4. **Culinary Delights:**

- The festival is synonymous with special dishes prepared using freshly harvested crops. Til (sesame) and gur (jaggery) are key ingredients in many sweets and snacks. Families come together to prepare and share traditional dishes, reinforcing the sense of community and togetherness.

Challenges and Opportunities

As with many traditional festivals, Makar Sankranti faces challenges in the modern era. Urbanization, changing lifestyles, and environmental concerns can sometimes impact the authenticity of celebrations. However, these challenges also present opportunities for communities to adapt and evolve, preserving the essence of the festival while making it relevant to contemporary values.

1. **Commercialization:**

- The commercialization of festivals is a common concern, with the focus shifting from traditional customs to consumerism. The sale of mass-produced kites, decorations, and sweets sometimes dilutes the authenticity of the celebrations. However, communities have the opportunity to support local artisans and businesses, promoting handmade and eco-friendly products.

2. **Environmental Impact:**

- The use of plastic and non-biodegradable materials in kite strings has raised environmental concerns. Communities are now exploring alternatives such as cotton strings and promoting responsible disposal of waste. The festival provides an opportunity to raise awareness about sustainable practices and environmental conservation.

3. **Preservation of Cultural Heritage:**

- In the face of globalization, there is a risk of losing some traditional customs and rituals associated with Makar Sankranti. However, communities and cultural organizations play a vital role in preserving and passing down these practices to future generations. Cultural programs, workshops, and educational initiatives can help maintain the rich heritage of the festival.

CONCLUSION

Makar Sankranti stands as a testament to India's cultural diversity, agricultural heritage, and spiritual traditions. It encapsulates the cyclical nature of life, celebrating the transition of the sun and the bounty of the harvest. The festival's ability to adapt to contemporary challenges while retaining its core values makes it a dynamic and living tradition.

As communities across India and the diaspora come together to celebrate Makar Sankranti, they weave a tapestry of customs, rituals, and shared joy. From the vibrant kites dotting the sky to the aroma of traditional dishes wafting through homes, Makar Sankranti is a sensory feast that engages the mind, body, and spirit. As the sun continues its northward journey, the festival serves as a reminder of the eternal cycles of nature and the interconnectedness of all living beings.

IX
CHRISTMAS

I will honour Christmas in my heart, and try to keep it all the year.

-Charles Dickens

Christmas: A Time of Tradition, Celebration, and Joy

INTRODUCTION

Christmas, one of the most widely celebrated festivals globally, holds a special place in the hearts of people from diverse cultures and backgrounds. Beyond its religious origins, Christmas has evolved into a season of joy, kindness, and shared festivities. This comprehensive exploration delves into the historical roots, religious significance, cultural expressions, and contemporary celebrations of Christmas, showcasing its profound impact on societies around the world.

Historical Roots

The historical roots of Christmas can be traced back to ancient times, with its origins entwined in both pagan and religious traditions. The celebration of the winter solstice, a time when days begin to lengthen after the darkest night of the year, was observed in various cultures. The Roman festival of Saturnalia, dedicated to the god Saturn, involved feasting, gift-giving, and a temporary suspension of social norms.

Christianity adopted and transformed these traditions, incorporating them into the celebration of the birth of Jesus Christ. The date of December 25th was chosen to coincide with existing festivities and to provide a Christian alternative to pagan celebrations. Over time, Christmas became a central event in the Christian liturgical calendar, observed by various denominations worldwide.

Religious Significance

At its core, Christmas is a Christian festival commemorating the birth of Jesus Christ. The biblical narrative, as recounted in the Gospels of Matthew and Luke, describes the miraculous birth of Jesus in Bethlehem. The event is marked by angelic announcements, the visit of the shepherds, and the arrival of the Magi, who brought gifts of gold, frankincense, and myrrh.

For Christians, Christmas is a time of spiritual reflection, expressing gratitude for the gift of Jesus Christ and the promise of salvation. Religious observances include midnight Mass, nativity scenes, carol singing, and readings from the Bible. The emphasis on love, compassion, and the message of peace on Earth resonates deeply with believers, fostering a sense of unity and spiritual renewal.

Cultural Expressions

While Christmas has its religious roots, it has transcended religious boundaries and become a global celebration embraced by people of various faiths and cultures. The fusion of religious and secular elements has given rise to a rich tapestry of cultural expressions, making Christmas a truly universal festival.

1. **Decorations and Christmas Trees:**

- The tradition of decorating homes with festive lights, ornaments, and Christmas trees has become synonymous with the holiday season. The evergreen tree, adorned with lights and decorations, symbolizes life, renewal, and the anticipation of the coming year. Communities and families gather to decorate their homes, creating a warm and festive atmosphere.

2. **Gift-Giving and Santa Claus:**

- The exchange of gifts during Christmas has deep historical roots, echoing the Magi's offerings to the infant Jesus. The modern figure of Santa Claus, inspired by the Dutch figure Sinterklaas, adds a whimsical element to the tradition. Children around the world eagerly await Santa's arrival on Christmas Eve, expecting gifts left under the Christmas tree or in stockings hung by the fireplace.

3. **Christmas Carols and Music:**

- Christmas carols, with their timeless melodies and lyrics, evoke a sense of nostalgia and joy. From classic hymns like "Silent Night" to lively tunes like "Jingle Bells," music is an integral part of Christmas celebrations. Community carol singing, concerts, and musical performances bring people together, fostering a sense of shared joy and camaraderie.

4. **Feasting and Special Foods:**

- Christmas is a time for feasting and indulging in special foods. Traditional dishes vary across cultures but often include roasted meats, festive desserts, and seasonal treats. The Christmas feast, whether a grand family gathering or a community potluck, is a symbol of abundance and shared joy.

5. **Nativity Scenes and Pageants:**

- Nativity scenes, depicting the birth of Jesus, are a common feature in homes, churches, and public spaces. Many communities organize live nativity pageants, reenacting the biblical story with participants donning costumes and portraying characters. These representations serve as visual reminders of the religious origins of Christmas.

6. **Light Displays and Parades:**

- Elaborate light displays, parades, and festive decorations transform cities and towns into enchanting wonderlands during the Christmas season. From twinkling fairy lights to extravagant displays of creativity, the visual spectacle of Christmas contributes to the festive ambiance and creates a sense of shared enchantment.

Regional Variations

Christmas is celebrated with diverse regional variations, each influenced by local customs, traditions, and cultural nuances. The way Christmas is observed in the snowy landscapes of Scandinavia differs from the sun-drenched festivities in Australia. These regional variations add unique flavors to the global celebration of Christmas.

1. **European Christmas Markets:**

- European countries, particularly Germany, are renowned for their enchanting Christmas markets. These markets, held in city squares, feature festive stalls selling handmade crafts, ornaments, and seasonal treats. Visitors can experience the magic of Christmas while enjoying mulled wine, roasted chestnuts, and the aroma of holiday spices.

2. **Las Posadas in Mexico:**

- In Mexico, the nine-day celebration of Las Posadas reenacts Mary and Joseph's journey to Bethlehem. Communities come together to participate in processions, seeking shelter in various homes. The celebration culminates in a feast, symbolizing the joyous arrival of the Holy Family.

3. **KFC Christmas in Japan:**

- In Japan, Christmas is not traditionally a religious holiday, but it is widely celebrated as a festive occasion. A unique tradition has emerged where people indulge in a Christmas meal from Kentucky Fried Chicken (KFC). The "Kentucky for Christmas" phenomenon has become a popular and quirky part of Japanese Christmas celebrations.

4. **Christmas in Australia:**

- Given that Christmas falls during the southern hemisphere's summer, Australians often celebrate with outdoor activities like barbecues, picnics, and trips to the beach. The visual contrast of traditional Christmas imagery with warm weather and summer activities adds a distinct charm to Australian celebrations.

Agricultural Dimensions

While not as explicitly tied to agriculture as some other festivals, Christmas does have agricultural dimensions. In the Northern Hemisphere, the winter season corresponds to a period of agricultural dormancy. Historically, the festive season provided an opportunity for communities to come together, share the bounty of the harvest, and engage in communal activities before the onset of harsh winter conditions.

The tradition of feasting during Christmas, with its emphasis on hearty and rich foods, reflects historical agricultural practices. In many cultures, the festive feast includes seasonal produce, such as winter vegetables and fruits, contributing to a sense of abundance and celebration.

Contemporary Celebrations

In the contemporary context, Christmas has evolved to embrace a myriad of expressions, influenced by cultural shifts, technological advancements, and changing societal dynamics.

1. **Technology and Virtual Celebrations:**

- The advent of technology has transformed how people celebrate Christmas, especially in the digital age. Families separated by distance can connect through video calls, exchanging festive greetings and sharing the joy of the season. Virtual events, online Christmas markets, and digital holiday cards have become integral aspects of contemporary celebrations.

2. **Commercialization and Consumerism:**

- The commercialization of Christmas is a topic of debate, with concerns about the emphasis on consumerism overshadowing the spiritual and cultural aspects of the festival. The holiday season often sees a surge in shopping, marketing campaigns, and the exchange of material gifts. However, communities and individuals can choose to focus on the spirit of giving, charitable endeavors, and meaningful experiences.

3. **Inclusive Celebrations:**

- Christmas has evolved to become an inclusive celebration, with people of various faiths and backgrounds participating in the festivities. Many secular aspects of Christmas, such as gift-giving, decorations, and festive meals, are enjoyed by people worldwide, contributing to a sense of shared cultural experience.

4. **Charitable Initiatives:**

- The Christmas season is synonymous with acts of kindness and charity. Many individuals and organizations engage in charitable initiatives, including food drives, toy donations, and support for those in need. The spirit of giving back to the community and helping those less fortunate is a central theme during Christmas.

Challenges and Opportunities

While Christmas brings joy and togetherness, it also faces challenges that resonate in the modern world. Balancing the traditional and spiritual aspects of the festival with the commercial and consumer-driven elements poses a continuous challenge. However, these challenges also present opportunities for individuals and communities to redefine the meaning of Christmas, emphasizing values of love, compassion, and community.

1. **Sustainability and Eco-Friendly Celebrations:**

- The environmental impact of Christmas, including excessive waste and energy consumption, is a growing concern. Communities and individuals are increasingly adopting eco-friendly practices, such as using sustainable decorations, minimizing single-use plastics, and supporting local and handmade products. This shift towards sustainability aligns with the broader global movement towards responsible consumption.

2. **Preserving Traditions and Cultural Heritage:**

- In the face of rapid cultural change, there is a need to preserve and promote traditional customs associated with

Christmas. Efforts to document, educate, and pass down cultural practices to future generations contribute to the richness and diversity of global celebrations.

3. **Balancing Tradition with Modernity:**

- Striking a balance between traditional celebrations and contemporary lifestyles poses a challenge. Families may grapple with the desire to uphold cherished customs while navigating the demands of a fast-paced and technologically driven world. Embracing new traditions while honoring the old allows for a dynamic and evolving celebration of Christmas.

CONCLUSION

Christmas, with its blend of religious roots, cultural expressions, and global significance, stands as a testament to the power of traditions to transcend boundaries and bring people together. Whether celebrated in the frosty landscapes of Europe, the sunny beaches of Australia, or the bustling streets of urban centers, Christmas retains its ability to evoke a sense of wonder, joy, and shared humanity.

As communities worldwide come together to celebrate Christmas, they contribute to a global tapestry of diverse customs and shared festivities. The spirit of Christmas, with its emphasis on love, generosity, and goodwill, resonates across cultures, making it a time for reflection, connection, and the celebration of the human spirit. In the twinkling lights, the sound of carols, and the warmth of festive gatherings, Christmas continues to weave its magic, reminding us of the enduring power of tradition and the universal desire for peace on Earth and goodwill toward all.

X
RAKSHA BANDHAN

May the thread of Rakhi always protect you and may our bond continue to flourish.

-Sadhguru Rai

Raksha Bandhan: A Sacred Thread of Love, Tradition, and Sibling Bond

INTRODUCTION

Raksha Bandhan, a festival deeply rooted in Indian culture, is a celebration of the unique bond between brothers and sisters. Observed on the full moon day of the Hindu month of Shravana, usually falling in July or August, Raksha Bandhan holds immense significance across India and among the Indian diaspora. This comprehensive exploration delves into the historical origins, religious and cultural significance, traditional rituals, contemporary celebrations, and the evolving nature of Raksha Bandhan.

Historical Origins

The historical origins of Raksha Bandhan are intertwined with legends and myths that have been passed down through generations. One such tale is that of the Mahabharata, the ancient Indian epic. According to the Mahabharata, Draupadi, the wife of the Pandava brothers, tore a piece of her sari and tied it around Lord Krishna's wrist to stop the bleeding. Touched by her gesture, Lord Krishna vowed to protect Draupadi in times of need. This narrative symbolizes the essence of Raksha Bandhan, where the thread (rakhi) becomes a symbol of protection and love.

Another legend associated with Raksha Bandhan is that of Queen Karnavati of Mewar, who sent a rakhi to Emperor Humayun, seeking his protection against the imminent invasion by Bahadur Shah of Gujarat. Touched by the queen's plea, Humayun set out to help her, marking the historical roots of Raksha Bandhan as a symbol of protection.

Religious Significance

Raksha Bandhan is deeply rooted in Hindu traditions, and its religious significance is reflected in the rituals and customs associated with the festival. The term "Raksha Bandhan" itself translates to "the bond of protection." The festival is a celebration of the bond between brothers and sisters, symbolized by the tying of a sacred thread, the rakhi, by the sister on her brother's wrist.

The ritual involves the sister applying a tilak (vermilion mark) on her brother's forehead, performing aarti (a ritual of waving a flame), and tying the rakhi while reciting prayers for the well-being and protection of her brother. In return, the brother offers a pledge to protect and support his sister throughout her life. The exchange of gifts further reinforces the bond, symbolizing love, care, and mutual respect.

While Raksha Bandhan is rooted in Hinduism, its celebration has transcended religious boundaries, with people of various faiths and communities participating in the festival, emphasizing the universal themes of love and protection.

Cultural Expressions

Raksha Bandhan is not just a religious occasion; it is a cultural celebration that permeates various aspects of Indian society. The festival is marked by colorful expressions of love, warmth, and familial ties.

1. **Rakhi Varieties and Designs:**

- The rakhi itself is a key element of the festival, and its design has evolved over time. Traditional rakhis were simple threads, but contemporary designs include intricate patterns, embellishments, and personalized touches. Rakhis now come in various materials, such as silk, zari, beads, and even ones incorporating modern elements like cartoon characters or pop culture references.

2. **Sweets and Gifts:**

- The exchange of sweets and gifts is a central feature of Raksha Bandhan. Brothers often present their sisters with jewelry, clothing, or items of personal significance. In return, sisters prepare special dishes or sweets for their brothers. This tradition fosters a sense of joy and celebration, with families coming together to share love and appreciation.

3. **Sibling Bond Celebrations:**

- Raksha Bandhan is a celebration of the unique bond between siblings. Brothers and sisters, whether biological or through close relationships, use the occasion to express their love and appreciation for each other. Families gather for meals, laughter, and the exchange of heartfelt sentiments, creating a warm and festive atmosphere.

4. **Long-Distance Celebrations:**

- In today's globalized world, where families may be dispersed across different cities or countries, Raksha Bandhan has adapted to accommodate long-distance celebrations. Sisters send rakhis by mail, and brothers reciprocate with virtual celebrations, connecting through video calls and online platforms to maintain the tradition despite physical distances.

Rituals and Traditions

The rituals associated with Raksha Bandhan are steeped in tradition, with each step carrying symbolic significance.

1. **Tilak and Aarti:**

- The sister begins the ritual by applying a tilak on her brother's forehead, symbolizing auspiciousness. Following this, she performs aarti, waving a flame in a circular motion around her brother, a gesture of protection and well-wishing.

2. **Tying of the Rakhi:**

- The centerpiece of the festival is the tying of the rakhi. The sister ties the sacred thread around her brother's wrist, symbolizing her love, trust, and the bond of protection. The act is accompanied by prayers for the brother's well-being and a promise of lifelong support.

3. **Exchange of Gifts:**

- After the rakhi is tied, the exchange of gifts takes place. Brothers give presents to their sisters as tokens of appreciation, and sisters reciprocate with love and affection. The gifts serve as tangible expressions of the bond shared between siblings.

4. **Feasting and Family Time:**

- The festivities extend to the dining table, where families come together to share a special meal. The joyous atmosphere is enhanced by the exchange of sweets, laughter, and the warmth of familial bonds.

Regional Variations

While the essence of Raksha Bandhan remains consistent, regional variations add diverse flavors to the celebration, reflecting the cultural tapestry of India.

1. **Raksha Bandhan in Northern India:**

- In North India, Raksha Bandhan is often celebrated with grandeur. Sisters may prepare elaborate meals for their brothers, and families come together for festive gatherings. The markets are adorned with colorful rakhis and sweets, creating a vibrant atmosphere.

2. **Rakhi Purnima in Odisha:**

- In Odisha, Raksha Bandhan is celebrated as Rakhi Purnima. The occasion is marked by sisters tying rakhis on the wrists of their brothers and performing rituals that include the application of tilak and aarti. The festival holds cultural and religious significance in the region.

3. **Narali Purnima in Maharashtra:**

- In Maharashtra, Raksha Bandhan coincides with the festival of Narali Purnima, which marks the beginning of the fishing season. Along with the traditional rituals of tying rakhis, coastal communities offer coconuts to the sea, seeking protection and prosperity.

4. **Rakhi Habba in Karnataka:**

- In Karnataka, Raksha Bandhan is known as Rakhi Habba. The rituals are similar, with sisters tying rakhis on their brothers' wrists. Additionally, some communities in Karnataka follow the tradition of 'Bhav Bij' where brothers visit their sisters' homes, bringing gifts and celebrating the bond.

5. **Jhulan Purnima in West Bengal:**

- In West Bengal, Raksha Bandhan is observed as Jhulan Purnima. Sisters tie rakhis on their brothers' wrists, and swings adorned with flowers are set up in homes and public spaces. The day is marked by devotional songs and cultural performances.

Agricultural Dimensions

Raksha Bandhan, while not directly associated with agriculture, is often timed to coincide with the monsoon season and the beginning of the sowing period in certain regions of India. As a festival that celebrates protection and the bond between siblings, it indirectly acknowledges the significance of a prosperous harvest and the well-being of family members engaged in agricultural activities.

The timing of Raksha Bandhan aligns with the agricultural calendar, creating a cultural bridge between urban and rural life. The festival brings a sense of joy and festivity to agrarian communities, marking a break in the agricultural cycle and providing an opportunity for families to come together.

Contemporary Celebrations

In contemporary times, Raksha Bandhan has evolved to adapt to changing lifestyles, technology, and societal dynamics. The essence of the festival remains intact, but new elements have been incorporated to make it relevant to modern sensibilities.

1. **Virtual Celebrations:**

- The advent of technology has facilitated virtual celebrations for those unable to be physically present with their siblings. Sisters send rakhis through postal services, and brothers reciprocate with video calls and online gift deliveries. Virtual celebrations allow families to bridge geographical gaps and maintain the tradition.

2. **Inclusive Celebrations:**

- Raksha Bandhan has become more inclusive, with the festival extending beyond biological siblings. Friends, cousins, and even non-family members participate in the celebration, emphasizing the universal theme of love, protection, and camaraderie.

3. **Customized Rakhis and Gifts:**

- The market for customized rakhis and personalized gifts has expanded, reflecting the contemporary trend of individual expression. Brothers and sisters seek out unique and meaningful ways to celebrate the occasion, incorporating personal touches that resonate with their relationships.

4. **Social Media and Raksha Bandhan:**

- Social media platforms have become a popular medium for sharing Raksha Bandhan celebrations. Families share pictures, videos, and messages, creating virtual albums that capture the festive spirit. The online space provides an avenue for extended family and friends to join in the celebrations, irrespective of physical distances.

Challenges and Opportunities

While Raksha Bandhan continues to be a cherished tradition, it faces certain challenges in the modern era. Balancing the sanctity of the festival with the demands of a fast-paced lifestyle and changing family structures presents both challenges and opportunities.

1. **Commercialization and Materialism:**

- The commercialization of festivals, including Raksha Bandhan, is a common concern. The emphasis on elaborate gifts and market-driven festivities can sometimes overshadow the core values of love, protection, and familial bonds. However, families have the opportunity to prioritize meaningful celebrations over materialism, emphasizing the emotional and spiritual aspects of the festival.

2. **Changing Family Dynamics:**

- With changing family structures and the geographical dispersion of family members, traditional celebrations may face challenges. Siblings residing in different cities or countries may find it challenging to be physically present for the rituals. However, this challenge also provides an opportunity for creative solutions, such as virtual celebrations and the exchange of digital sentiments.

3. **Preserving Cultural Heritage:**

- The fast-paced nature of modern life may contribute to a gradual erosion of cultural traditions. Preserving the rich heritage of Raksha Bandhan involves efforts to educate younger generations about the significance of the festival, encouraging them to value and participate in its traditions.

4. **Gender Sensitivity:**

- In recent years, there has been a growing awareness of the need for gender sensitivity in the way Raksha Bandhan is portrayed and celebrated. While traditionally the festival involves sisters tying rakhis on their brothers' wrists, contemporary perspectives highlight the importance of mutual protection and respect in sibling relationships, regardless of gender.

CONCLUSION

Raksha Bandhan, with its deep historical roots, religious significance, and cultural expressions, stands as a timeless celebration of love, protection, and familial bonds. The festival has evolved over the centuries, adapting to changing societal dynamics while retaining its core values. Raksha Bandhan serves as a reminder of the enduring importance of family, love, and the unique bond shared between siblings.

As the sacred thread of the rakhi is tied, and the rituals unfold, Raksha Bandhan creates moments of joy, reflection, and connection. Whether celebrated in the traditional setting of a family home, the vibrant atmosphere of Indian markets, or through virtual means in the global diaspora, Raksha Bandhan transcends borders and unites people in the shared celebration of love and protection.

In a world marked by constant change, Raksha Bandhan remains a beacon of cultural continuity, weaving the threads of tradition into the fabric of contemporary life. As families come together to celebrate this auspicious day, they contribute to the enduring tapestry of Indian culture, fostering a sense of unity, resilience, and the timeless beauty of sibling bonds.

XI
JANMASHTAMI

May Lord Krishna's flute invite the melody of love into your life. May Radha's love teach not only how to love but to love eternally!

-Arup Singhania

Janmashtami: Celebrating the Birth of Lord Krishna

INTRODUCTION

Janmashtami, also known as Krishna Janmashtami or Gokulashtami, is a Hindu festival that marks the birth of Lord Krishna, an incarnation of Lord Vishnu. Celebrated with great fervor and devotion across India and among the global Hindu community, Janmashtami falls on the eighth day (Ashtami) of the dark fortnight in the Hindu month of Bhadrapada, usually in August or September. This comprehensive exploration delves into the historical roots, religious significance, cultural expressions, traditional rituals, regional variations, and contemporary celebrations of Janmashtami.

Historical Roots

The historical roots of Janmashtami are deeply embedded in the sacred texts of Hinduism, particularly in the epic narrative of the Bhagavad Gita and the Mahabharata. Lord Krishna, the eighth avatar of Lord Vishnu, is believed to have been born in Mathura to Vasudeva and Devaki, who were imprisoned by Devaki's brother, the tyrannical King Kansa. Fearing a prophecy that predicted his demise at the hands of Devaki's eighth son, Kansa imprisoned his sister and her husband.

The story of Janmashtami takes a divine turn with the miraculous birth of Lord Krishna in the prison cell. According to the narrative, Lord Krishna was born at midnight in the month of Bhadrapada. In an extraordinary sequence of events, Vasudeva miraculously carried the newborn Krishna across the flooded Yamuna River to the safety of Gokul, where he was raised by Nanda and Yashoda, foster parents.

The childhood exploits of Lord Krishna, including his playful encounters with gopis (milkmaids) and the divine episodes of the Ras Leela, are celebrated as part of the Janmashtami festivities. The festival encapsulates the divine playfulness, wisdom, and compassion embodied by Lord Krishna.

Religious Significance

Janmashtami holds immense religious significance for Hindus, as it commemorates the appearance of Lord Krishna on Earth. Lord Krishna is revered as the Supreme Being, the source of divine knowledge, and a guide to righteous living. The Bhagavad Gita, a sacred scripture within the Indian tradition, is a conversation between Lord Krishna and the warrior Arjuna, taking place on the battlefield of Kurukshetra. In this discourse, Lord Krishna imparts profound spiritual wisdom and teachings on duty, righteousness, and devotion.

The festival is a time for devotees to reflect on these teachings and seek inspiration from Lord Krishna's life. Midnight prayers, recitation of hymns, and the singing of bhajans (devotional songs) are common religious practices during Janmashtami. Temples dedicated to Lord Krishna witness an influx of devotees, and the deity is adorned with special decorations and clothing to mark the auspicious occasion.

Cultural Expressions

Janmashtami is not only a religious festival but also a celebration of culture, art, and devotion. Various cultural expressions manifest during the festivities, contributing to the vibrancy of the celebration.

1. **Rasa Lila and Folk Dances:**

- The Rasa Lila, a traditional dance depicting the divine love between Lord Krishna and the gopis, is a cultural expression deeply associated with Janmashtami. In addition to classical dance performances, folk dances like the Raas Leela in Gujarat and the Dahi Handi celebrations in Maharashtra showcase the rich tapestry of Indian cultural expressions.

2. **Decorations and Temples:**

- Homes and temples are adorned with vibrant decorations, including flower garlands, rangoli (colored powders arranged in patterns), and images depicting scenes from Lord Krishna's life. Temples dedicated to Lord Krishna become focal points of celebration, with elaborate decorations, processions, and special events.

3. **Devotional Music and Bhajans:**

- Devotees engage in singing bhajans and devotional music dedicated to Lord Krishna during Janmashtami. These melodious expressions of devotion create a spiritual ambiance and bring communities together in worship.

4. **Theatrical Performances and Plays:**

- The life of Lord Krishna, especially his childhood exploits, is often dramatized through theatrical performances and plays. These performances, known as Krishna Leela or Bal Leela, captivate audiences and bring the stories of Lord Krishna to life.

Traditional Rituals

Janmashtami is marked by a series of traditional rituals that vary across regions but generally revolve around fasting, prayers, and the observance of nocturnal rituals.

1. **Fasting and Ekadashi:**

- Many devotees observe a fast on Janmashtami, abstaining from food and water until midnight, the supposed time of Lord Krishna's birth. The day before Janmashtami, known as Ekadashi, is often observed as a day of heightened spiritual practices and a prelude to the festive celebrations.

2. **Midnight Aarti and Abhishek:**

- The midnight hour, believed to be the time of Lord Krishna's birth, is a sacred moment during Janmashtami. Devotees gather at temples to participate in the midnight aarti, where lamps are lit, hymns are sung, and prayers are offered. The deity is often bathed in a ritual known as abhishek, symbolizing the purification and celebration of the divine birth.

3. **Swinging of the Cradle (Jhulanotsava):**

- In some regions, a cradle with an idol of baby Krishna is adorned, and devotees take turns swinging it gently. This ritual, known as Jhulanotsava, symbolizes the joyous occasion of Lord Krishna's birth and the expression of devotion by his followers.

4. **Dahi Handi Celebrations:**

- In Maharashtra, the Dahi Handi festival is a major highlight of Janmashtami. Young men, known as Govindas, form human pyramids to break a suspended pot filled with curd, butter, and other goodies. This tradition recreates Lord Krishna's mischievous childhood act of stealing butter from hanging pots.

Regional Variations

Janmashtami is celebrated with unique regional variations, reflecting the diversity of Indian culture. Each region adds its distinct flavor to the festivities, incorporating local customs and traditions.

1. **Gopalkala in Maharashtra:**

- In Maharashtra, a special dish called Gopalkala is prepared as an offering to Lord Krishna. It typically consists of flattened rice, curd, jaggery, coconut, and green chilies. The Dahi Handi celebrations, as mentioned earlier, are an integral part of Janmashtami in Maharashtra.

2. **Raas Leela in Gujarat:**

- Gujarat is known for its vibrant celebration of Janmashtami, with the Raas Leela dance being a central feature. Devotees form circles and dance to the rhythmic beats, depicting Lord Krishna's divine love for Radha and the gopis.

3. **Jhulan Yatra in West Bengal:**

- In West Bengal, Janmashtami is celebrated as Jhulan Yatra. Devotees set up swings and cradles adorned with flowers, and idols of Radha and Krishna are placed on them. The swinging of the deities symbolizes the divine couple's romantic playfulness.

4. **Sri Krishna Jayanti in South India:**

- In South India, especially in states like Tamil Nadu and Karnataka, Janmashtami is celebrated as Sri Krishna Jayanti. The festival involves elaborate processions, decorations, and the singing of bhajans in temples. Special prayers and discourses on the Bhagavad Gita are organized.

Agricultural Dimensions

While not directly associated with agriculture, Janmashtami often aligns with the agricultural calendar in India. The festival falls during the monsoon season, a crucial time for farmers when sowing of crops is underway. The celebration of Janmashtami provides a break from the agricultural routine, allowing communities to come together, offer prayers for a bountiful harvest, and seek divine blessings for the well-being of their crops.

The imagery of Lord Krishna as a cowherd, playing his flute amidst lush green landscapes, resonates with the agrarian context of rural India. The festival serves as a cultural bridge between urban and rural communities, creating a sense of shared joy and celebration during the agricultural cycle.

Contemporary Celebrations

In contemporary times, Janmashtami has evolved to adapt to changing lifestyles, urbanization, and global influences. While traditional rituals remain integral, new elements have been incorporated to make the festival relevant to modern sensibilities.

1. **Cultural Programs and Competitions:**

- Schools, colleges, and cultural organizations organize Janmashtami events, including cultural programs, dance performances, and competitions. These events provide a platform for the younger generation to connect with their cultural heritage and showcase their talents.

2. **Krishna Costume Contests:**

- Krishna costume contests are popular, especially among children. Participants dress up as Lord Krishna or Radha, adorned with colorful attire and accessories, adding a playful and festive dimension to the celebration.

3. **Digital Celebrations:**

- In the era of digital communication, Janmashtami celebrations extend to online platforms. Temples livestream midnight aartis, and virtual events allow devotees from around the world to participate in the festivities. Social media platforms also play a role in sharing greetings, images, and devotional messages.

4. **Community Service and Philanthropy:**

- Many individuals and organizations use Janmashtami as an opportunity for community service and philanthropy. Food drives, charity events, and donations to the less fortunate are common during the festival, aligning with the principles of compassion and selfless service embodied by Lord Krishna.

Challenges and Opportunities

While Janmashtami continues to be a significant cultural and religious celebration, it faces certain challenges in the modern era. The delicate balance between traditional values and contemporary influences, as well as the commercialization of festivals, poses both challenges and opportunities.

1. **Commercialization and Festive Commodification:**

- The commercialization of festivals, including Janmashtami, has raised concerns about the commodification of religious and cultural practices. The emphasis on marketing products, elaborate decorations, and commercial events sometimes overshadows the spiritual essence of the festival. However, communities have the opportunity to prioritize the intrinsic values of devotion, simplicity, and community over materialism.

2. **Preserving Authenticity and Tradition:**

- With the pace of modern life, there is a risk of diluting the authentic traditions associated with Janmashtami. Efforts to preserve and promote traditional rituals, devotional practices, and cultural expressions are essential for maintaining the festival's richness and authenticity.

3. **Inclusivity and Outreach:**

- Janmashtami provides an opportunity for inclusivity and outreach, embracing people of all backgrounds and age groups. Initiatives that engage the youth, promote cultural awareness, and foster a sense of community contribute to the relevance and continuity of Janmashtami.

4. **Environmental Sustainability:**

- The use of eco-friendly materials and sustainable practices in decorations and celebrations is a growing concern. Communities can adopt environmentally friendly alternatives, reducing waste and contributing to the broader movement towards sustainability.

CONCLUSION

Janmashtami, with its rich historical roots, religious significance, cultural expressions, and traditional rituals, stands as a vibrant celebration of Lord Krishna's divine life. As families and communities come together to observe the festival, they create a tapestry of devotion, cultural pride, and shared joy.

In the rhythmic beats of folk dances, the fragrance of incense in temples, and the colorful decorations adorning homes, Janmashtami resonates with the heartbeat of Indian culture. Whether celebrated in the traditional setting of a temple, the fervor of a cultural event, or the warmth of a family gathering, Janmashtami encapsulates the timeless spirit of devotion and the eternal playfulness of Lord Krishna.

As India and the global Hindu diaspora immerse themselves in the festivities of Janmashtami, they weave a narrative that transcends time and space—a narrative that echoes the teachings of the Bhagavad Gita and the enduring legacy of Lord Krishna. In the celebration of Janmashtami, the divine and the human converge, creating a moment of transcendence where devotees connect with the eternal wisdom and love embodied by the divine child, Krishna.

XII
ONAM

May the vibrant colors of Onam fill your life with joy and happiness.

-Shekar Reddy

Onam: Embracing Tradition, Culture, and Harvest Celebrations in Kerala

INTRODUCTION

Onam, the vibrant and culturally rich festival of Kerala, holds a special place in the hearts of its people. This annual harvest festival, celebrated with unparalleled enthusiasm and fervor, marks the homecoming of the mythical King Mahabali. Observed in the Malayalam month of Chingam, usually falling in August or September, Onam is a reflection of Kerala's unique cultural heritage, rich traditions, and the spirit of unity and festivity. This comprehensive exploration delves into the historical origins, religious and cultural significance, traditional rituals, elaborate festivities, regional variations, and contemporary celebrations associated with Onam.

Historical Origins

Onam is deeply rooted in mythology and is associated with the legendary King Mahabali, a benevolent and just ruler. According to Hindu mythology, Mahabali, also known as Maveli, was a powerful and virtuous king who ruled over Kerala. His reign was marked by prosperity, justice, and the well-being of his subjects.

Despite his virtuous rule, Mahabali's success became a concern for the gods, particularly Lord Indra. Feeling threatened, Indra sought the assistance of Lord Vishnu, who took the form of Vamana, a dwarf Brahmin, to curb Mahabali's influence. Vamana approached Mahabali, who was known for his generosity, and requested a small piece of land that he could cover in three steps. The benevolent king agreed, unaware that Vamana's steps would encompass the entire universe.

In a divine gesture, Vamana transformed into a giant and covered the entire earth and sky in two steps. For the third step, Mahabali offered his own head, displaying unparalleled devotion and sacrifice. Touched by Mahabali's unwavering commitment, Vamana granted him a boon – the opportunity to visit his kingdom and people once a year.

This annual homecoming of King Mahabali is celebrated as Onam, and it is believed that during this time, the spirit of the king returns to Kerala, bringing joy and prosperity to the land.

Religious and Cultural Significance

Onam is primarily a Hindu festival, but its significance transcends religious boundaries, encompassing cultural, social, and historical dimensions. The festival embodies the spirit of unity, secularism, and the harmonious coexistence of diverse communities in Kerala.

1. **Hindu Mythological Significance:**

- Onam is linked to Hindu mythology, particularly the legend of King Mahabali and Vamana. The festival is a celebration of Mahabali's virtuous rule, his devotion to the divine, and the spirit of sacrifice. Devotees believe that Mahabali's annual visit during Onam brings prosperity, abundance, and well-being to the land.

2. **Cultural Heritage:**

- Onam is a manifestation of Kerala's rich cultural heritage, showcasing traditional art forms, music, dance, and culinary delights. The festival provides a platform to express and preserve the unique customs and traditions that define the cultural identity of the state.

3. **Secular Celebration:**

- While Onam has Hindu origins, it is celebrated by people of all faiths in Kerala. The festival's inclusivity and secular nature reflect the diversity and tolerance ingrained in Kerala's social fabric. Onam transcends religious boundaries, fostering a sense of unity and shared celebration.

4. **Harvest Festival:**

- As a harvest festival, Onam is a time to celebrate the bountiful harvest and express gratitude to nature for its abundance. The festival marks the end of the monsoon season, and the lush green landscapes of Kerala come alive with colorful decorations, traditional rituals, and joyous celebrations.

Traditional Rituals

Onam is characterized by a series of traditional rituals and customs that add depth and meaning to the festivities. These rituals are observed with great reverence, connecting the present generation with the age-old customs of their ancestors.

1. **Atham and Athapookalam:**

- Onam celebrations kick off with the auspicious day of Atham in the Malayalam month of Chingam. The traditional flower carpet, known as Athapookalam, begins on Atham and continues to grow in size over the ten days of the festival. Each day, additional layers of flowers are added to the intricate design, creating a vibrant and colorful display.

2. **Thiruvonam Day:**

- The most significant day of Onam is Thiruvonam, which is considered the day of King Mahabali's return. Devotees wake up early, take a ritual bath, and wear new clothes. Traditional rituals include preparing a grand feast known as Onasadya, visiting temples, and participating in cultural events.

3. **Onasadya – The Grand Feast:**

- Onasadya is a sumptuous feast served on banana leaves, featuring a variety of traditional dishes. The feast typically includes rice, sambar, avial, olan, thoran, pickles, and a plethora of desserts. The elaborate meal is a symbol of abundance and prosperity, and families come together to share the feast, reinforcing the sense of community and togetherness.

4. **Pulikali – Tiger Dance:**

- Pulikali, meaning "play of the tigers," is a traditional dance form performed during Onam. Men dressed as tigers paint themselves with vibrant colors and perform energetic and rhythmic dances. This lively and entertaining art form adds a dynamic and playful element to the festivities.

5. **Vallam Kali – Boat Race:**

- Vallam Kali, or snake boat race, is an integral part of Onam celebrations in some regions of Kerala. Teams of oarsmen row long, narrow boats decorated like snakes in a spirited competition. The boat races attract large crowds, adding an element of excitement and sportsmanship to the festival.

Elaborate Festivities

Onam is not just a one-day affair but a ten-day extravaganza that unfolds with various activities, cultural events, and community engagements. The festive spirit engulfs Kerala, transforming it into a vibrant and joyful spectacle.

1. **Pookalam – Floral Carpet Competition:**

- Creating intricate and colorful flower carpets, known as Pookalam, is a competitive and artistic event during Onam. Communities, schools, and households participate in Pookalam competitions, showcasing their creativity and floral arrangement skills. The designs often feature intricate patterns, mythological themes, and vibrant color combinations.

2. **Cultural Programs and Competitions:**

- Onam is a time for cultural performances, including classical dances, music concerts, and drama presentations. Various competitions, such as folk dance contests, boat race championships, and traditional sports events, are organized to engage the community and showcase local talent.

3. **Traditional Attire:**

- Traditional attire adds to the festive ambiance of Onam. Men often wear the traditional Mundu and Veshti, while women don the elegant Kasavu sarees. The traditional clothing, combined with elaborate jewelry and accessories, contributes to the visual splendor of the celebrations.

4. **Processions and Parades:**

- Onam processions featuring decorated elephants, folk artists, and cultural floats are organized in different parts of Kerala. These grand parades, known as Onam Pageantry, showcase the diverse cultural heritage of the state and attract large crowds.

5. **Cultural Exhibitions:**

- Onam exhibitions, known as Onakalikal, showcase traditional arts and crafts, handloom products, and local cuisines. These exhibitions provide a platform for artisans and craftsmen to display their skills, promoting the rich cultural tapestry of Kerala.

Regional Variations

While the essence of Onam remains consistent across Kerala, regional variations add diverse flavors to the celebration. Different communities within the state may incorporate unique customs and traditions, making Onam a festival that reflects the cultural diversity within Kerala.

1. **Thrikkakara Appan Onathappan in Central Kerala:**

- In the central region of Kerala, particularly in and around Thrikkakara, the focus is on the deity Vamana, one of the incarnations of Lord Vishnu. Devotees offer special prayers and celebrations center around Thrikkakara Appan, a manifestation of Vamana.

2. **Vallam Kali in Alappuzha and Kottayam:**

- Vallam Kali, or boat races, are particularly popular in the districts of Alappuzha and Kottayam. The snake boat races draw massive crowds, and each boat is a symbol of community unity and skill.

3. **Pulikali in Thrissur:**

- Thrissur is known for its exuberant Pulikali performances during Onam. The lively and colorful tiger dance is a major attraction, featuring vibrant costumes and energetic performances.

4. **Kummati Kali in Palakkad:**

- Kummati Kali, a traditional folk dance, is popular in the Palakkad region. Men dressed in colorful attire and wearing masks perform this rhythmic dance, adding a distinct cultural touch to Onam celebrations.

5. **Kaikottikali and Thumbi Thullal in Malabar Region:**

- The Malabar region, in the northern part of Kerala, celebrates Onam with unique dance forms such as Kaikottikali and Thumbi Thullal. Kaikottikali involves women dancing in a circle, clapping their hands in sync with the rhythm, while Thumbi Thullal is a traditional dance performed by women.

Contemporary Celebrations

In contemporary times, Onam has evolved to adapt to changing lifestyles, urbanization, and global influences. While traditional rituals and customs remain at the core, new elements have been incorporated to make the festival relevant to modern sensibilities.

1. **Digital Celebrations:**

- The advent of technology has facilitated virtual celebrations for those unable to be physically present for Onam. Online platforms and social media play a significant role in connecting families and friends, allowing them to share greetings, images, and messages despite physical distances.

2. **Onam in the Diaspora:**

- The Keralite diaspora around the world actively participates in Onam celebrations, creating a sense of connection to their cultural roots. Onam events, including cultural programs, feasts, and competitions, are organized in various countries with significant Keralite populations.

3. **Inclusive Celebrations:**

- Onam has become more inclusive, with people of diverse backgrounds and communities participating in the festivities.

Cultural exchange programs, where individuals from different regions showcase their traditional arts and cuisines, contribute to a broader and more diverse celebration.

4. **Sustainable and Eco-Friendly Initiatives:**

- In recent years, there has been a growing awareness of the need for sustainable and eco-friendly celebrations. Efforts to promote the use of natural and biodegradable materials in Pookalam designs, reduce waste during festivities, and adopt eco-friendly practices are gaining momentum.

Challenges and Opportunities

As Onam continues to be a symbol of Kerala's cultural richness, it faces certain challenges in the modern era. The delicate balance between preserving traditions and adapting to contemporary influences presents both challenges and opportunities.

1. **Commercialization and Materialism:**

- The commercialization of festivals, including Onam, is a concern for those who wish to preserve the festival's cultural and spiritual essence. The emphasis on elaborate decorations, consumerism, and market-driven festivities can sometimes overshadow the intrinsic values of community, togetherness, and gratitude.

2. **Preserving Traditional Arts:**

- Traditional art forms, such as Pulikali and Vallam Kali, face the challenge of maintaining their authenticity and popularity in the face of changing tastes and preferences. Efforts to preserve and promote these art forms involve imparting training to new generations and creating platforms for artists to showcase their talents.

3. **Environmental Conservation:**

- As Onam involves elaborate decorations, feasts, and cultural events, there is a need for heightened awareness about environmental conservation. Initiatives to reduce waste, promote eco-friendly practices, and emphasize sustainability can contribute to the long-term well-being of the festival and the environment.

4. **Cultural Awareness and Education:**

- Ensuring that younger generations understand the cultural significance and traditions associated with Onam is crucial for its continuity. Educational programs, cultural events in schools, and community initiatives can play a pivotal role in fostering awareness and appreciation among the youth.

CONCLUSION

Onam, with its historical roots, religious and cultural significance, traditional rituals, elaborate festivities, regional variations, and contemporary adaptations, stands as a symbol of Kerala's cultural vibrancy. As families and communities come together to celebrate the festival, they create a tapestry of colors, traditions, and shared joy that resonates with the spirit of Onam.

In the rhythmic beats of traditional dances, the aroma of Onasadya wafting through homes, and the vibrant designs of Pookalam adorning courtyards, Onam encapsulates the essence of gratitude, unity, and cultural pride. Whether celebrated in the traditional setting of a family home, the grandeur of a boat race, or the warmth of a community gathering, Onam transcends boundaries, creating a moment of collective joy and cultural continuity.

CONCLUSION

Festivals are occasions to empower ourselves in the course of humanity

-Sudhir Verma

Conclusion: The Rich Tapestry of Festivals in India

India is a land of myriad festivals, a vibrant tapestry woven with threads of cultural diversity, religious fervor, and historical significance. Each festival celebrated in this country carries a unique narrative, symbolizing traditions, beliefs, and values that have been passed down through generations. The festivals of India are not merely events on the calendar; they are reflections of the nation's soul and a testament to its enduring cultural heritage.

In this essay, we have explored some of the most prominent festivals celebrated in India, each offering a glimpse into the diverse facets of the country's rich and complex culture.

From the exuberant colors of Holi to the sacred lamps of Diwali, from the grand processions of Eid to the spiritual fervor of Guru Nanak Jayanti, these festivals mirror to the many faces of India.

Cultural Unity Amidst

One of the most remarkable aspects of India's festival landscape is the coexistence of a multitude of traditions and beliefs. Despite the staggering diversity in languages, religions, and regional customs, festivals have an exceptional ability to unite people. They transcend the boundaries of caste, creed, and social status, bringing communities together in a harmonious celebration of life.

India's festivals foster a sense of unity and brotherhood. Regardless of the specific festival, the underlying message is often one of hope, renewal, and the triumph of good over evil. It is a message that resonates with people from all walks of life, reminding them of the common values that bind them together as Indians.

Religious Significance and Spiritual Reflection

The festivals of India are not just occasions revelry; they are deeply rooted in religious traditions and hold profound spiritual significance. Whether it's the devotion and penance of Lent during Easter, the self-for discipline of fasting during Ramadan, or the contemplative prayer during

Buddha Purnima, these festivals provide a platform for spiritual reflection and growth.

The rituals and practices associated with these festivals provide an opportunity for believers to reconnect with their faith and strengthen their relationship with the divine. These moments of introspection are essential for personal growth and the development of a moral and ethical compass.

Festivals as a Reflection of History and Mythology

India's festivals are also a window into the country's rich history and mythology. The stories and legends behind these festivals are deeply intertwined with the country's past, often representing the struggles and triumphs of legendary figures, as well as the enduring traditions and customs of different communities.

For example, the grand celebration of Durga Puja in West Bengal marks the triumph of the goddess Durga over the demon Mahishasura, reflecting the theme of good prevailing over evil. In contrast, the commemoration of Eid al- Adha resonates with the willingness of Prophet Ibrahim to sacrifice his son, Isma'il, as an act of obedience and devotion.

Economic and Societal Impact

India's festivals are not just spiritually and culturally significant; they also have a substantial impact on the economy and society. The economic significance of these festivals cannot be underestimated. They driveconsumer spending, boost sales in various sectors, and provide employment opportunities for artisans, craftsmen, and the service industry.

Furthermore, festivals promote a sense of community and social bonding. They encourage interaction between people, regardless of their backgrounds, and promote a spirit of togetherness. Whether it's celebrating the arrival of Lord Ganesha during Ganesh Chaturthi or sharing the joy of Eid al- Fitr with neighbors, these festivals contribute to social cohesion and a sense of belonging.

Challenges and Concerns

While India's festivals are moments of joy and celebration, they are not without challenges and concerns. Some of these issues have come to the forefront in recent years:

1. **Environmental Impact**: The grand scale of festival celebrations can sometimes lead to adverse environmental consequences. For example, the immersion of idols made of non-biodegradable materials during Ganesh Chaturthi

can pollute water bodies. There is a growing awareness of the need for eco-friendly practices to mitigate these environmental impacts.

2. **Safety and Crowd Management**: The massive influx of people during festivals can lead to issues of safety and crowd management. Ensuring the security of participants and preventing accidents is a significant concern.
3. **Noise and Air Pollution**: The use of firecrackers and loudspeakers during festivals contributes to noise and air pollution, which can affect public health. This has led to discussions about regulating these activities and promoting quieter and more eco-friendly alternatives.
4. **Commercialization**: The commercialization of festivals, driven by consumerism, can overshadow their spiritual and cultural significance. Finding a balance between tradition and materialism is a challenge that society faces.

Preserving Traditions in a Changing World

India's festivals are continually evolving to adapt to the changing times. In a globalized world, where traditions are constantly being reshaped, it is essential to preserve the authenticity and cultural significance of these festivals. At the same time, it is equally important to find ways to make these celebrations relevant to new generations while respecting the core values and beliefs.

In this regard, many festivals in India have shown remarkable adaptability. For instance, Diwali and Eid celebrations have transcended geographical boundaries and are now celebrated by Indian diaspora communities worldwide, creating a sense of continuity and belonging for those living far from their homeland.

The Message of Unity and Tolerance

India's festivals, with their diverse traditions and customs, reflect a message of unity and tolerance. They demonstrate that in the face of differences, humanity can come together in celebration, mutual respect, and shared values. They show that it is possible to find common ground, even in a country as diverse as India, and to celebrate this unity amidst diversity.

India's festivals are a reminder that the nation's strength lies in its unity, its traditions, and its ability to embrace the richness of its cultural mosaic. These festivals teach us the importance of respecting one another's beliefs, upholding our traditions, and fostering a society where everyone can celebrate their faith and culture without fear or prejudice.

In conclusion, the festivals of India are a testament to the country's rich history, its diverse culture, and its enduring values. They offer a unique glimpse into the heart of the nation and the soul of its people. These festivals are more than just rituals; they are moments of celebration, reflection, and unity. They are a source of joy, inspiration, and a reminder of the unifying power of humanity's shared traditions and values.